"I have learned a vast amount about implementing clean growing techniques from Zac. His years of experience are evident in every explanation about proper pest and disease prevention and treatment. Zac is someone you want on your side."

— **Paul Valenzuela, The Clone Coach**
CloneCoach

"Having a reliable source for help is vital to success. Zac is the person I go to whenever an issue arises. His IPM knowledge is vast. He's helped us through a couple of really tough situations, saving us time and money. On top of that, he's developed a strategy to keep our garden clean and pest-free. Whether you have a specific problem you're dealing with or you need a great IPM strategy, Zac is the person you want on your side! They say "an ounce of prevention is worth a pound of cure". Follow Zac's advice, he'll save you and your pounds."

— **Damian Deforest**, President
Apex Extracts

"I've had the privilege of working with Zac for quite a few years now. Zac has provided critical support. Every time I get to work with Zac I'm enlightened, and inspired to keep learning. Having him as a resource is something I'll forever be grateful for."

— **Nicholas Rees**, General Manager/Creator
StackHouse Nevada

"I have known Zac for years and his scientific approach to cannabis has always inspired me as a grower. His suggestions have changed the way I see my rooms."

– Dylan Kohagen, Head Grower
ARTSY

"Zac's love for the plant and passion for cultivating clean cannabis is second to none. His willingness to share the plethora of knowledge he has gained throughout the years—with the grower's success at heart—proves his commitment to his craft."

– Kalen Bigg, Manager
ACW Supply

Zac Ricciardi & Ben Owens

CLEAN GROWING:
INTEGRATED PEST MANAGEMENT FOR CANNABIS GROWERS

Owens Holdings LLC

First published by Owens Holdings LLC 2024

Text & Cover Design by: Ben Owens

ISBN-13: 978-1-7332099-5-3 (Paperback)

First Edition

Do it right, or don't do it.

Clean Growing

Integrated Pest Management

for Cannabis Growers

ZAC RICCIARDI
BEN OWENS

Table of Contents

INTRODUCTION

Let's face it: IPM isn't fun, it's necessary.

"IPM is the red-headed stepchild of the cannabis industry," as Zac likes to say.

Before Zac Ricciardi ever worked in cannabis, he wanted to be a skateboarder, and, at the age of 17, he moved to San Francisco—a skateboarding mecca—to chase that dream.

It was there that he found a thriving cannabis culture unlike anything he had ever experienced. So, in a way, we can all thank skateboarding for bringing a resource like Zac to this space.

Zac's journey would take him from trimming in Mendocino, to growing and processing in San Diego and Santa Cruz, where he saw firsthand the potential this industry had, as well as its need for SOPs that helped growers prevent problems and save crops.

After moving to Colorado, Zac oversaw a hydroponics store while working with several large grows, helping growers develop and implement IPM SOPs that allowed them to be successful.

As his knowledge and experience increased, Zac was brought on as the National Cannabis Specialist for BioSafe Systems, visiting grows and helping growers from coast-to-coast.

One of these facilities belonged to ETHOS Genetics, which is where Zac and Ben's paths crossed.

Around this time, Ben was a Senior Staff Writer with The Hemp Connoisseur magazine, and had just profiled Colin Gordon, ETHOS' founder, for the Spring 2020 issue. This piece led to a series of co-authored articles designed to help growers get more out of their gardens.

In 2021, Colin introduced Ben to Zac, his go-to IPM resource—someone you could count on for help with all things pests, pathogens, and problems.

Over the course of the next few years working and writing together, Zac became a close friend and an invaluable resource.

Fireside Chats

Most people can't just call up Zac and ask for help.

Before the lockdowns of the pandemic, Zac was a regular speaker at trade shows and grow events, spreading knowledge and fielding questions from hobby and commercial growers alike. But, without in-person events, he had to get creative.

So, "Fireside Chats" were born thanks to social media.

By Summer of 2022, Zac had recorded more than 40 of these live videos, leading growers of all levels through an IPM masterclass.

The problem?

The platform.

Videos are great, and we HIGHLY recommend doing a deep dive on these fireside chats if you have the time and interest (it's basically a free class that will save you $1000s).

But, when you're in the grow, and you have an issue, you need a solution fast.

You don't have time to scroll through 40 videos to find what you're looking for.

So, in October 2022, Zac and I discussed the idea of him writing a book on IPM that growers could keep on the shelf in the grow for quick, easy access and actionable guidance.

As a published author and veteran journalist who applied his degrees to the newly-legal cannabis industry, Ben's career has been dedicated to helping professionals like Zac share their value and expertise.

For over a decade, Ben has profiled countless cannabis founders, growers, and innovators, helping piece together their mistakes, lessons, and advice in a way that is accessible to interested readers.

While Zac visits 100s of grows every year, he can't be everywhere, but his expertise can.

The goal was simple:

Capture the wealth of information that Zac had shared with growers, boiling it down into an actionable guide for everyday use in any grow.

Give growers a tool for preventing and fixing problems in the grow that saved them the embarrassment of asking for help, and the costs of trying to figure it out on their own.

When we have a problem in the grow, the last thing most of us want to do is tell someone about it.

Too often, this leads to the wrong solutions for the wrong diagnoses.

This book aims to help with that.

How This Book Will Benefit You

The most experienced growers will tell you that you need to experience the pains of pest infestations and pathogen outbreaks in order to feel confident dealing with them in the future. Like many, Zac and I have had to learn many of these tactics the hard way, and from personal experience, we can say that having the tools in advance sure makes it easier to push through.

At some point, every grower is forced to make a choice: abandon ship, or batten down the hatches.

If you're here, we assume you're not the quitting type (which is good, because if you are, this is certainly not the book for you).

Without the right processes in place, tools on hand, and knowledge of what to do, pests and pathogens can destroy months of hard work (and millions of dollars of product).

In the pages that follow, Zac and I will break down some of the most common issues you'll encounter when growing cannabis, as well as step-by-step processes you can use in your grows—from small tent grows to large commercial operations.

While science supports what is written in this book, this is far from an academic paper; it's a manual, to be used as a quick-reference guide for insight and practical guidance.

The fields that IPM draws on—chemistry, biology, horticulture, and more—have been around for many years in other agricultural industries. This book offers a synthesis of this information to be used specifically for cannabis cultivation.

Our hope is to provide you with the information you need to feel confident preventing, detecting, and addressing threats in your grow.

CHAPTER ONE

10 Habits Of Highly Successful Cultivators

How To Address Issues Before They Become Problems

Growers of all skill levels can benefit from a sense of preparedness.

Being prepared starts with having a plan, and having the right tools and people in place to follow that plan. In our experience working with cultivators of all skill levels in licensed and hobby grows, these are proven habits that will help you be as successful as possible.

The 10 Habits of Highly Successful Cultivators

1. Be proactive, not reactive.

Have plans in place for anything that could go wrong and know what you are going to do if issues arise. This includes not only your processes but also an understanding of who can help you if things go wrong.

2. Don't just show up on time, be early.

Farming is one of those things where issues can arise at any given point. Having enough time in the day to take care of whatever may happen is going to be to your benefit.

3. Spend wisely and reserve resources.

Spending your money wisely will allow you to be successful in and out of the grow. Avoid overspending on one component

18

of the garden at the expense of another. Make sure you have a reserve of resources available to you in case things don't go as planned.

4. Establish and use SOPs (Standard Operating Procedures).

The most successful gardeners that we work with don't have gardeners, they have SOPs. SOPs allow for replicable results, and fine-tuning of your processes.

In a grow, SOPs are your chosen path. They can give you a routine to follow that is consistent, which allows you to better understand the impact of changes you make in that process, or can offer a Plan B if you are experimenting with new variables.

(A good rule of thumb is that your SOPs should be thorough and simple enough that any non-grower could follow the steps.)

5. Read as often as you can about cultivation.

There is a ton of really good information out there that will allow you to further your knowledge base and make you a better grower. Go beyond instagram and look at the published research and data coming out of universities around the country and world. There is a wealth of knowledge in studies that have been done overseas on hemp and related crops that is all pertinent to what we do daily in our grows.

Regularly reading research will further your ability to be successful.

6. Don't be afraid to ask questions.

There are no stupid questions, only stupid mistakes.

Before you implement a procedure or process, make sure that you not only know **what you are doing** but **why you are doing it**, so if anything needs to be modified, you are able to do so efficiently.

7. Know the grow from the ground up.

Whether you are a Hobby Grower or the facility head of the commercial facility you own, know your facility from the ground up.

There shouldn't be anywhere in your grow that you haven't seen personally. This is especially true if your grow is your livelihood.

Knowing your grow in and out will make troubleshooting and maintenance that much easier if you end up managing an issue.

8. Implement and maintain a maintenance plan in your grow.

Grows are full of Limited Lifespan Supplies; things that are "soft goods" like bulbs, filters, containers, sprayers, or anything that needs maintenance.

Establishing and following a maintenance plan will maximize the longevity of your equipment (so that you get the most out of your investment), as well as avoid unexpected delays because you don't have the right tool or part.

If you take care of your equipment, your equipment will take care of you.

9. Have extras of everything.

Not being able to do basic tasks-like transplant, flip, or clone-because you don't have the right (or enough) supplies is a huge hit.

Tracking your Supply Burn Rate (how fast you use how many supplies) will give you the ability to forecast and order what you need well before a need becomes urgent. If you have the ability, buy extra or double, and store the rest so that you always have a reserve, but don't overspend and hurt your reserves (see #3).

Having a space where you can keep back stock is a great idea, especially in today's society with the supply issues we have.

By doubling up on supplies like media, irrigation components, IPM supplies, nutrients, and anything you use regularly, you'll never get caught without the necessary equipment.

10. Know (and train) your team.

As a Grower, your team includes your peers and co-workers, but also:

- Mentors - Those who help you along the way.
- Experts - Those you turn to for a specific category of advice.
- Fellow Growers - Those who share advice, as well as help with plant-sitting and genetic preservation.

Not everyone needs to know (or have access to) everything, but redundancy is key.

If something happens and you are unable to attend to your grow (due to injury, illness, work, vacation, etc.), having someone who is familiar with your setup and willing to assist allows you to plan for and pivot when situations arise.

It is for this reason that many growers share specific cuts with one another in an effort to backup genetic stables in case you lose a plant.

You don't need everyone to know how to do everything, but it's definitely good to have a backup in every situation.

Just like extra components, having a team that can step into fulfill different roles as needed will allow you to be that much more successful.

The #1 Rule of Highly-Successful Growers: *Keep things proactive rather than reactive to address issues before they every become problems.*

CHAPTER TWO

The Pest-Pathogen Triangle

The 3 Key Elements Pests & Pathogens Need To Thrive

Something that comes up often when dealing with pests or pathogens is "The Pest-Pathogen Triangle".

In short, a pest or pathogen scenario relies equally on three factors:

1. Susceptible Host
2. Pest-Pathogen Pressure
3. Conducive Environment

The Pest-Pathogen Triangle

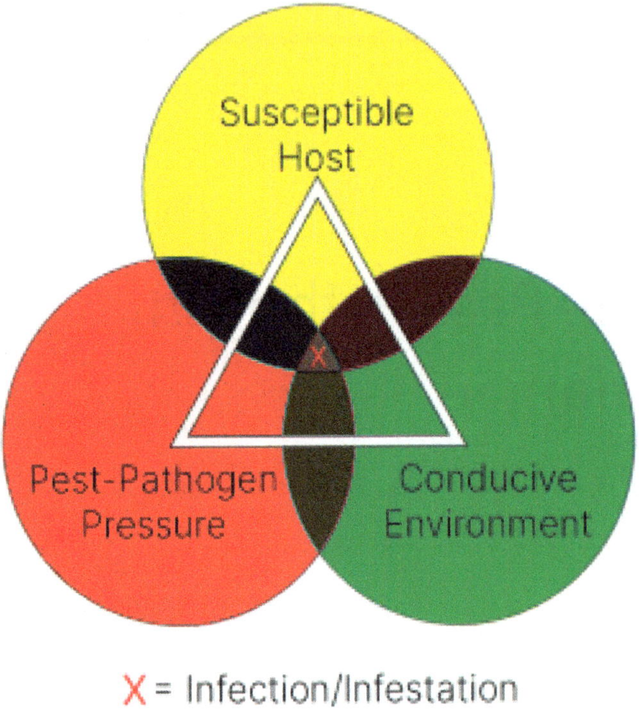

Any infection scenario is going to need all three key factors for it to be an issue in your garden.

Susceptible Hosts

The relationship between pests and pathogens, and susceptible hosts follows the natural law of order: predators go after the weakest prey.

Pest and pathogen pressures are always present. But if the situation is right (conducive environment) and the prey is within reach (susceptible), the predator will strike. Predators rarely go after prey that is going to be a challenge for them, and a strong host presents a challenge compared to sick, weak, or old alternative with less resources to fight back.

Promoting optimal plant health allows you to eliminate the Susceptible Host variable as best as possible.

You can do this naturally by ensuring plants are fed properly, as well as with supplemental support such as plant health products that promoted induced systemic response (ISR), the plant's natural defense against threats. Good rhizosphere health, with plenty of microbial activity, will encourage beneficial microorganisms to work with your plants.

If your plants are as healthy as possible, they're much less likely to be susceptible hosts.

Conducive Environment

Pests and pathogens need the right environment to prosper.

Some environments breed more issues than others, that's just how it goes. Having proper control over your space and implementing proactive spray regiments will be key for you if you are in a naturally conducive environment. This includes areas with large temperature fluctuations, as well as exceedingly humid environments.

Proper moisture levels and airflow are essential to controlling your environment.

Monitor your environment to ensure that you don't have giant spikes in temperature and humidity in your grow. Ensure that you are encouraging your growing media to dry before saturating with feeds; periodic dry downs can mitigate root zone issues found in excess moisture. Good ventialtion and circulation both above and below the canopy will prevent stagnant air and moisture pockets where issues can breed.

Monitoring your grow's air quality, temperature, and humidity levels will help to eliminate conducive environments where threats thrive.

Every threat needs a sweet spot to start to take over your space. If you avoid that sweet spot by promoting a healthy plant and treating the environment, you're going to see significantly less instances of infestation and infection.

Pests & Pathogens

Bad News: There are spores and pests around us at all times.

You can't get away from pest and pathogen pressures.

They're in our garbage. They're on our pets. They're in the air around us.

The question is whether our environment is conducive and our host susceptible enough to allow these threats to take hold?

It's that overlap in the middle of all three where infection occurs. Proper IPM and scouting is critical; the proactive approach is always better than a reactive one.

Quick & Easy Preventative Recommendations:

Even if you don't have an issue, employ an IPM Strategy (prevent and prepare for issues rather than react to them).

This holds true for both pests and pathogens.

For pests, I always recommend incorporating AzaGuard into your preventative SOP:

- Even if you don't see bugs, a preventative spray of AzaGuard will mitigate any insects that could find their way in
- AzaGuard prevents pests from being able to efficiently latch onto and feed from your plants, making it harder for them to establish themselves (and an infestation) in your space.
- Any time you are doing preventative sprays, make sure that AzaGuard is part of that rotation.

For pathogens like molds and mildews, you want to employ tools that are both preventative as well as curative.

Utilize products like OxiPhos and Zerotol on a 3-week rotation to give you a desired ISR and ensure that if there are any spores floating around that they are not able to take hold (because we have eliminated their ability to procreate freely).

If you can address the susceptible hosts and make sure that your environment is on point, and are regularing scouting and spraying for pests and pathogens, you can mitigate most issues before they become problems.

CHAPTER THREE

Induced Systemic Response (ISR)

What It Is, Why It's Important, And How To Use It To Our Advantage

When you think of Induced Systemic Response (ISR), think of it like a plant's "immune system;" ISR is the response a plant elicits when threatened.

Similar to your body getting a flu shot or experiencing a fight-or-flight event:

- A threat is presented
- Your body calls its troops to arms
- And goes to work fighting that threat off in a heightened state of defense

Now, imagine that you can elicit that response without a threat actually being present.

Your plant is on hyper-alert for any threat, all hands on deck, and ready to destroy the first hint of an enemy.

That's what ISR is; it's telling the plant to turn all of its defense mechanisms on, even when there isn't a threat, so that it operates as if it must protect itself and its health at all costs, all the time.

A plant with an active ISR won't get caught off guard by a surprise attack; it'll be ready.

The Importance of ISR

Like your body knowing how to fight off the flu, your plant's systems know how to fight off threats, but they don't naturally kick in until those threats are present.

It's like having body armor but not putting it on until people are shooting at you. Helpful, but not as helpful as if you'd had it on preventatively, just in case.

A healthy body is hard to infect, and a healthy plant is the same way.

A plant with a strong, active ISR will be less likely to be a susceptible host, removing one of the key elements of the triangle needed for a threat to survive.

Using ISR To Our Advantage

Aside from infecting your plants (which would no doubt cause an ISR but also an infection), you can trick your plants into thinking a threat is present when it isn't.

Products like OxiPhos use a potassium phosphite to elicit an ISR response without a threat actually being present. Once activated, the ISR that OP elicits lasts for 21-days (3 weeks)

That's 3 weeks that your plant is on guard, ready for whatever.

And, if you're running a 9-week cycle, that means you can apply OP every 3 weeks, from moms to clones to veg to flower and ensure that first line of defense is strong and consistent.

A strong ISR is great for rooted plants, but also helps susceptible plant tissue (like cuttings before they root) stay protected and healthy throughout the process.

We'll talk about ISR frequently throughout this book, and teach you how to use it to your advantage, but the basics are:

1. ISR is a natural plant defense mechanism
2. It's harder to attack a plant whose defenses are active
3. You can elicit ISR chemically without a threat present
4. Doing so gives you up to 3 weeks of protection and stronger clones

CHAPTER FOUR

The 4 Pathogen Families in Cannabis

What They Are, How They Spread, and How to Protect Your Crop

Pathogens strike fast and spread rapidly, especially in an industry like cannabis.

Like any crop, pathogens in cannabis can spread through your growing medium, tools, shared water reservoirs, and even the grow's air. Being able to identify these pathogens before the spread will save your harvests, and ensure a clean final product.

Three out of four pathogens are curable.

Bacterial, fungal, and oomycota pathogens can all be eliminated from a grow even after an infection has taken hold; viral pathogens, on the other hand, are nearly impossible to fully eliminate.

The 4 Pathogen Families in Cannabis

1. Bacterial Pathogens

Most commonly seen as rots and blights, bacterial pathogens start from bacterial cells found throughout a grow space.

Method of Spread:

- Mechanical (shared tools, such as scissors used to defoliate multiple plants)
- Surface (trays, pots, and tables)
- Water (shared reservoirs, runoffs, trays)

Treatment Options:

1. **Plant Tissue: Zerotol + OxiPhos Combo.** Disinfest with a high level disinfectant and encourage Induced Systemic Response (ISR) from the plant to fight off infection.

2. **Hard surfaces: Sanidate 5.0.** Food-safe sterilization and comprehensive on-label treatment of bacterial pathogens.
3. **Preventative: Guarda.** Thyme-oil-based, preventative polymer used in growing media to prevent rot or blight by infiltrating bacterial cells before they become self-sustaining spreaders.

2. Fungal Pathogens

The most common fungal pathogens in cannabis and hemp crops include *fusarium*, *verticillium*, *septoria*, and mildews, and are spread by active or dormant (resting) spores.

Method of Spread:

- Mechanical
- Air
- Water
- Plant Debris
- Growing Media (Substrate)

Treatment Options:

1. **Plant Tissue: Zerotol 2.0 or HC.** High level disinfectant treatment known to cure fungal pathogens on plant tissue.
2. **Hard surfaces: Sanidate 5.0.** Food-safe sterilization and comprehensive on-label treatment of fungal pathogens.

Because spores can be present anywhere, disinfesting is paramount to preventing and treating fungal pathogens.

3. Oomycetes (Oomycota)

Oomycetes are a little-known but detrimental group of fungus-like organisms that reproduce both sexually and asexually through the development and exchange of spores (zoospores and oospores). Common Oomycota include downy mildew, pythium, and phytophthora.

Like fungal pathogens, oomycota spores can be present almost anywhere.

Method of Spread:

- Air
- Plant Debris
- Growing Media (Substrate)

Treatment Options:

1. **Plant Tissue: Zerotol 2.0 or HC.** High level disinfectant treatment known to attack oomycota on plant tissue. Add OxiPhos for additional ISR support.
2. **Hard surfaces: Sanidate 5.0.** Food-safe sterilization and comprehensive on-label treatment of bacterial pathogens.

3. **Preventative: Remove old debris from the grow.** The less debris you've got around, the less chance of encouraging spore spread.

4. Viral Pathogens

The least treatable of the bunch, the most common viral pathogens in cannabis are Tobacco Mosaic Virus (TMV) and Hops Latent Viroid (HpLVd) and spread through virus RNA, often spread through contamination.

There are no known cures for infected plant material as of this writing, though various tissue culture methods that can be used to propagate new plants from uninfected tissue.

Method of Spread:

- Insect
- Mechanical
- Plant Debris

Treatment Options:

1. **Plant Tissue:** The only know treatment for viruses in cannabis is extreme disinfesting, typically not recommended for plant tissue. Even then, you are not really able to completely eliminate the virus from the plant's tissue.

2. **Hard surfaces: Sanidate 5.0.** Food-safe sterilization and comprehensive on-label application for viral pathogens.
3. **Preventative: Remove affected plants from the grow and avoid bringing in untested cuts.** Viruses and viroids can even spread in latent (non-expressing) stages. Healthy plants may not show signs that they are carriers for these pathogens. Shared reservoirs (I.e. aerocloners) and shared runoff in trays (even if a plant is asymptomatic) can spread these viruses to other genetics in your grow.

We have heard anecdotal evidence that a combination of Zerotol and OxiPhos can suppress viral symptoms, but the pathogen itself remains present, and is merely a band-aid for a bullet wound to get you to the finish line.

Your best approach to pathogens is to prevent the spread before it starts. Viruses spread exponentially and compromise entire gardens quickly.

When in Doubt:

- Ditch affected plants
- Maintain a disinfested environment
- Avoid cross-contamination.

CHAPTER FIVE

Powdery Mildew 101

Scout, Prevent, And Cure

Powdery Mildew is one of those problems that, when left unchecked, only gets worse over time.

It's also everywhere.

You'd be hard pressed to find an environment that is free from spores.

Powdery Mildew shows up in the wild as well as in home gardens. It's a safe bet to assume there is always some chance of those spores being present.

That's why knowing what prevention and curative processes we can employ if it does find its way into the garden will allow us to promptly address and stay ahead of it in the future.

Powdery Mildew, commonly known as PM, is a common issue that indoor, outdoor, and greenhouse growers experience, and it is one of those threats that can pop up overnight.

The longer you leave it unchecked, the worse the damage will become.

In the following pages, we're going to cover:

- How To Scout For PM (what to look for & what situations it's most likely to appear)
- Preventative & Curative Processes
- Remediation (Preventing future PM Outbreaks in previous outbreak environments)

How To Scout

Luckily, PM is fairly easy to identify by its circular white appearance.

When scouting for PM, look at both canopy leaves as well as leaves that may be shaded from light or blocked from air circulation.

These are most likely to have stagnant pockets of humidity and temperature, and can be sources of PM infestations.

Additionally, if your grow or facility experiences a large swing in temperatures or humidity—due to a power outage, severe weather, or equipment failure—you will want to pay extra

42

attention when scouting as these conditions can encourage those spores to take hold and spread fast.

PM is something that can be gotten rid of; it's not a death sentence. But knowing what to look for, and having processes in place to cure and prevent it will make the difference in your outcome.

Preventative & Curative Processes

Processes exist to help you address and prevent PM outbreaks.

If we think about traditional agriculture, things like cucumbers or tomatoes, those growers also have crops that are susceptible to PM, and if they have an outbreak they can't just cut everything down and start over. They have to be able to get rid of it with the proper rotation of products and come out on top, which means you can, too.

To treat for PM before you even have it, use a rotation of a disinfestant and something that elicits that ISR in your crop.

We recommend using ZeroTol 2.0 and OxiPhos.

You want to use those two together because the peroxyacetic acid (PAA) component of ZeroTol is going to allow you to have a higher level of disinfesting than the OP would on its own.

The OP's potent combination of peroxide and mono and dipotassium salts of phosphoric acid allows you to elicit an ISR from your plants, accomplishing 2 things at once.

With this combination, you are disinfesting that mycelium in the canopy while eliciting ISR, giving those plants an additional 21-day boost in protection against PM hyphae.

APPLICATION PROCESS: Treat 1x every 21-Days

1. Mix ZT and OP together at a 1:300 rate each (about 13ml/gal).
2. Treat your mother plants before you take your clones.
3. Treat your veg plants.
4. Hit them again when you flip.
5. Then again in Week 3 of flower.
6. Then again in Week 6.

Note: You can use ZT at 1:256 for spot treatments during that 21-day time period between applications.

Assuming that you are running a 9-week cycle (for flower), that will basically take you from propagation to harvest with that ISR.

This heightens your plants' ability to fight off certain fungal pathogens and diseases it could encounter, including PM. In the case of PM, this process is going to allow the plant to keep PM hyphae from taking hold.

If we look at how powdery mildew functions:

- It's a little spore that's floating around

- Then, it lands on your leaf tissue
- Then, it penetrates your leaf tissue, with something similar to a root called a hyphae

Once that hyphae is put into that cellular tissue, you need to use something like OxiPhos or Regalia or a similar product that engages a plant's own defense system to fight said hyphae.

If we only treat the surface of that leaf tissue, that hyphae continues to exist.

Think of it like a dandelion:

If you cut a dandelion at ground level, but you leave the root zone intact, every time that dandelion comes back it's going to be a little more established, a little more voracious. That's because that "root zone" has been allowed to expand.

PM is very similar.

If a hyphal protrusion is present in that cellular tissue, then your hyphae will continue to propagate and your infection—in terms of the actual visible PM—is going to get much worse.

OP helps that plant take care of that hyphae so it's not something that keeps coming back.

The other option for growers is to basically remove the affected tissue, but in some situations, you can't take the entire plant off the stalk because you won't have anything left to grow.

So, that Systemic Acquired Response (SAR)/Induced System Response (ISR) option is very important for cannabis growers because it works without leaving anything behind that would ever make a grower fail for testing (because, again, it is potassium phosphite). It is just a PK molecule that plants can't regulate the uptake on, which is what elicits that ISR and allows a plant to use its own defense system to fight off pathogens.

Note: Some strains are more susceptible to PM than others.

We've found that varieties that are high in limonene and pinene appear to be less susceptible, which possibly has something to do with the antiseptic properties of those terpenes and their natural ability to fight off things like mold and mildew.

The fruitier strains seem to be more susceptible.

PM is an environmentally-exacerbated issue.

If you're in a warehouse in an area like CO, chances are you're going to see PM flare up in the spring, fall and winter where we have very cold nights and warm days.

Like the glass of ice water on a hot day, when that condensation occurs and we increase that relative humidity, that's when you're really going to see PM start to germinate.

Let's say you have a corner in the back of the room where the airflow isn't as good as it necessarily could be, and that plant is always a bit more susceptible.

During that 21-day period between applications, it is acceptable to go in there and spray ZeroTol as a spot treatment on that area or plant, but I would not recommend using that OP again

OP's 21-day residual is a stress response, so more is not necessarily better with that product.

If you stress out a plant more than it needs to be to elicit that response in a positive manner, then you can actually cause undue stress, which is going to be counter-productive. Adhere to the 21-day interval with OP, and use ZeroTol as needed at 1:256.

PM likes humidity; it likes stagnant, moist areas without much airflow.

Environment plays a huge role in PM, so proper air flow and defoliation are key components of prevention.

Making sure plants are properly cleaned up will assist in making sure that PM doesn't come back if you've had it before. Air flow and desiccation helps mitigate any of those residual spores that could be in the garden that find their way in.

The more air flow you can get into the environment, the less you are going to see this pathogen and the easier it will be to get rid of.

Post-Outbreak Remediation

After you've addressed an outbreak, your next biggest priority is to prevent another.

Once you have disinfested with something like ZT, it's not a bad idea if your environment is less than preferable to follow up with an inhibitor like citric acid, sodium bicarbonate, or potassium bicarbonate, as well as certain bacillus products.

With a clean slate, you can put down an inhibitor and prolong that period between sprays, allowing you to go as much as 50% longer between applications.

Your goal at this point is to keep threats from getting back in there and re-propagating and doing their thing, and the longer you maintain that clean slate, the easier that will be.

These are great tools for growers that may have a less than preferable environment, or for growers that are just dealing with changes in weather patterns.

If it's rainy and cold the day after it was warm, and you're growing in a hoop house, go spray some ZeroTol today as a preventative to make sure that if any environmental situations pop up that could encourage growth that you are staying ahead of the situation.

Aside from disinfesting and inhibition, the third key approach to preventing future outbreaks is focusing on proper airflow—both ventilation and circulation.

In this case, if your intake and exhaust are functioning properly, you'll want to focus on circulation to mitigate stagnant pockets and microclimates within your canopies.

There is an awesome company called Vosterman that makes a product called a V-Flow fan and it helps encourage a process called destratification. Destratification acts like a typical water fountain; it takes the air from the floor and circulates it back down, similar to a fountain (there's tons of cool videos of this process online).

For PM, being able to equalize your environment and have the same relative humidity at the ceiling as at the floor, and have the temperature consistent, is going to result in you seeing much less instance of things like PM breaking out.

Plus, it'll help with other molds and mildews like botrytis, which are also encouraged by environmental swings.

CHAPTER SIX

Botrytis 101

What It Is, How It Spreads, and How to Treat It

Botrytis is a fungus that affects yields (and profitability) of both indoor and outdoor grows.

Botrytis, more commonly known as "bud rot" is an anaerobic pathogen that survives in conducive, low-oxygen conditions that allow the pathogen to grow.

A nice full cola is going to be the perfect environment for botrytis to take off. Once those fungal spores are in the cola, it can decimate an entire floret making it unsellable.

The worst part about botrytis is that it often goes undetected until a plant has been harvested.

Part of getting rid of Botrytis is making sure that you don't have it. Doing regular maintenance is crucial. Make sure you're pruning as needed and doing your due diligence with scouting (more on that later).

Where does Botrytis Grow?

Botrytis is an anaerobic fungus that grows from the inside out.

It's hard to see if you have it, but there are a two telltale signs:

- **Calyx Prematuration:** One (or more) parts of your flower already has orange, crispy hairs, and others may be yellow (an indicator that it might be Botrytis)
- **Caterpillars:** If you grow outside and see caterpillars, caterpillars defecate where they eat. When they are pooping inside buds, they create that perfect environment for Botrytis to take hold. Caterpillars and botrytis go hand in hand, so, if you see caterpillars, it's a good idea to do a preventative botrytis treatment.

Botrytis is most common in the fall, when the days are hot and the nights are cool.

Temperature swings allow the pathogen to take advantage of "morning dew"-moisture from the evening. This humidity spike, coupled with heat of day, can encourage microbial growth inside colas.

The key to dealing with nature's temperature and humidity swings is being diligent with your preventative efforts.

The Best Ways to Treat Botrytis

1. A Combination of a nonionic surfactant and a sterilizing agent.

- Use a nonionic surfactant such as Coco Wet, Thermax 70, Natural Wet. You want something that is going to be able to permeate into the cola.
- Combine that with Zerotol 2.0 or HC for the contact sterilization.

2. Get your grow on a 3-Week rotation of Bactericide/Fungicide like OxiPhos that elicits an Induced Systemic Response.

- Healthy plants are less susceptible to disease.
- If you can keep an ISR going from regular applications, you will see less instance of Botrytis in your susceptible varieties

Keep in mind - the anaerobic aspect of this pathogen is what makes it treatable.

If we are able to get in there with nonionic disinfest product and ZeroTol 2.0 (1% solution, 1:100; 37ml/gal), and soak all the way into the stem, we can sterilize the entire floret and all tissue in between, making sure that Botrytis isn't allowed to linger and continue to perpetuate.

Chem-Free Botrytis Hack: Popsicle Sticks

The thing we recommend doing—and in some situations it is next to impossible by sheer crop volume—is using wooden popsicle sticks to open airways in your colas.

We have all been to the doctor and had the tongue depressor popsicle sticks; you can get these at your local hobby store.

For varieties you know are susceptible, take that stick and break it at a 45° angle, and then pull open the cola, and stick the 45° section in against stem so it will hold the bud open from the main cola so you and actually get oxygen in there.

For an infection to exist you need a conducive environment, a threat, and susceptible host, and this removes the conducive environment part of triangle.

The environment makes it so Botrytis isn't able to propagate correctly; We are basically desiccating it through air circulation, complementing our disinfesting sprays so it doesn't come back.

In humid environments, it is advantageous to scout for Botrytis early.

If you live in places like New England or the Pacific Northwest (PNW), botrytis can be a frequent threat. It used to happen to Zac in Santa Cruz when he lived there and is definitely something you have to plan for.

Botrytis can develop after you've already harvested.

Make sure that you are properly disinfesting your rooms–both grow and dry/cure rooms–in between efforts to ensure you have disinfected for residual yeasts, molds, and fungi that could be left over from previous crops.

It would be unfortunate to get everything right until the cure and, at the very last stage, have a pathogen affect your yields.

Making sure your cure rooms are clean is paramount to finishing strong, and we'll touch more on pre- and post-cycle disinfesting in a later chapter.

For now, while there are multiple ways to disinfest your rooms, the most effective is to disinfect the entire space with a food grade disinfectant like Sanidate 5.0 before the crop goes into the room, and then follow up with sulfur packets like Gard'nclean during the curing process to make sure there's no residual contamination from employees coming in and out or other vectors of spread.

When Botrytis comes around, having a game plan in place is the best way to protect your crops and ensure successful yields that allow you to continue on into the next year or cycle.

CHAPTER SEVEN

Common Pests in Cannabis & How To Treat

Fungus Gnats, Root Aphids, Russet Mites, & Spider Mites

Pests can infiltrate, reproduce, and wreak havoc as fast (or faster) than pathogens.

They spread rapidly, especially in an industry like cannabis where plants, genetics, and growers regularly change environments.

"Hitchhikers" as they are often called, pests can be brought in on clothing, clones, substrates, tools, and anything that is used from one environment to another.

Being able to identify and treat these pests before they reproduce and cause an infestation will save your harvests, and ensure a clean final product.

Pests are curable in most cases without having to sacrifice the entire crop.

Common pests like fungus gnats, root or canopy aphids, and spider mites can all be treated without having to nuke your garden. Other pests, like Russet Mites, can take more extreme efforts to catch, contain, and prevent future infestations.

For every pest, it's important to be able to:

- Properly **identify** what the pest is (so you aren't treating the wrong thing)
- Correctly **treat** using a process and chemistry designed for that pest (so you aren't using the wrong tools for the job)

Treating for Fungus Gnats in Cannabis 101

Sciarid flies, better known as fungus gnats, are pests that feed on decaying material in your grow and can quickly become a nuisance.

The best approach to combating fungus gnats is a combination of specific plant chemistries and clean cultural practices.

First, you want to remove the conducive environment from the equation.

If you can take away the conducive environment part of the triangle, you take away their happy home.

Removing the conducive environment for fungus gants is a three-pronged approach of dry downs, food removal, and grow cleanliness.

1. Dry Downs

The first thing I recommend looking at with any fungus gnat infestation are your dry-down practices:

- How often are you getting adequate dry downs?
- Do you completely saturate your media or use intermittent irrigation?
- What is the moisture content of your media?
- What are you growing in?

The answers will directly affect the decomposition of your media.

When it's wet, your media starts to decompose, and what do fungus gnats eat? Decaying organic material.

Dry downs have a direct correlation on fungus gnat populations.

2. Removal of Food Source

In addition to managing your dry downs, disinfesting your media eliminates decaying material that fungus gnats feed on.

If they don't have a food source, they can't stick around.

We recommend Zerotol 2.0 or Zerotol HC for disinfesting grow media.

Keeping things clean and sterile will further reduce your pest population.

3. Clean Grow

Don't forget to clean up the entire grow or facility; decaying debris anywhere is a potential conducive environment for a pest problem.

Make sure you are regularly removing debris from the grow, trash containers, and the surrounding areas.

Again, fungus gnats feed on decaying material.

Dead leaves on tops of your pots and trays-or being tracked in and out of the grow on the floor-can all increase the likelihood of fungus gnats.

Fungus Gnat IPM

The most common methods for tracking and treating Fungus Gnats are a combination of passive and mobile pesticides.

Passive Pesticides: Sticky Cards & Diatomaceous Earth (DE)

The implementation of sticky cards and DE can be very effective for fungus gnats.

It is important to keep in mind that sticky traps have grids so that they can be used as monitors; Sticky cards alone will not cure a fungus gnat infestation.

If you can no longer keep track of how many gnats are on your cards, it's time to replace them.

I like to use these in combination with mobile pesticides because passive pesticides are immobile and rely on insects having to come across them to be effective.

Active Pesticides: Insecticides & Mycoinsecticides

An active pesticide is one that is going to be applied intermittently and targets pests whether they are moving or not.

I recommend AzaGuard® and/or BioCeres® WP for this purpose.

Natural Predators: Nematodes

The other thing that a lot of growers have found to be very beneficial is the introduction of nematodes in conjunction with AzaGuard or BioCeres applications.

Certain species of nematodes can be very effective against fungus gnat larvae.

The goal of your process is to target pests at all stages of life, in both the root zone and the canopy.

Incorporating a drench process is not hard to do and compounds your spray efforts by going after gnats and larvae in the root zone.

Insecticides like AzaGuard have an antifeedant quality that discourages pests from feeding, which affects their ability to molt (mature), further reducing the population.

If your pests cannot get to an adult stage, they cannot procreate.

Add in the power of a mycoinsecticides like BioCeres whose ovicidal properties impact the ability of larvae to hatch, and your fungus gnat population starts rapidly shrinking.

BioCeres is an entomopathogenic soil-borne fungus that is very effective against soft bodied insects such as fungus gnat larvae and can also be used to target root aphids.

Being able to find and have products that provide you more than one level of control is essential to a strong IPM process.

3-Step Fungus Gnat IPM:

1. Take away food source.
2. Mess with molt.
3. Prevent reproduction.

Following this process will allow you to get rid of any fungus gnat infestation you encounter.

A Note on Fungus Gnats & Pythium

Fungus gnats often hang out where pythium may be; they have the same conducive environments.

Going back to what we learned about common pathogens, Pythium is a parasitic oomycete that can cause root rot, leading to further issues in your garden.

One does not necessarily mean the other is present, but they go together like PB&J, and if you see one, you likely have the other.

By disinfesting your media and removing decaying organic matter that fungus gnats feed on, you are simultaneously addressing any pythium symptoms you may encounter by keeping things nice and sterile.

For this reason, Zerotol is a great 1-2 punch that you can deliver to both gnats and pythium in the same applications, eliminating the conducive environment variable from the triangle.

Aphids or Gnats? Identifying Your Pests

A lot of growers out there have dealt with fungus gnats or root aphids, and many may have been unknowingly dealing with them.

There's a lot of misinformation out there when it comes to differentiating between the two.

Here's what you need to know so that you can properly identify, treat, and prevent further issues.

If you asked most growers what the difference is visually between gnats and aphids, they couldn't tell you, and that's a problem because if you can't identify what's wrong, you're gambling with treatment options hoping something lines up (which is a waste of time and money).

64

There are three things to look at:

- Body Structure
- Wingspan to Body Ratio
- Petioles

The first thing to think about when dealing with fungus gnats or root aphids is the body structure.

Root aphids will look bulbous, without a defined abdomen or thorax.

Fungus gnats, like mosquitos, have a clearly defined thorax, and a body style that differentiates it from an aphid once it has reached its second life stage.

As they get older, the larger wings of a root aphid are a dead giveaway.

- A root aphid's wingspan will be longer than (sometimes double) its body.
- Fungus gnats are the opposite, with a wingspan much closer in proportion to the pest's body.

In the root zone, you don't (shouldn't) have any flyers, so you need to look at the body structure.

If you've caught it early and you aren't dealing with flying pests, you'll need to look for cornicles coming out of a root aphid's backend (often referred to as "tailpipes").

Fungus gnats do not have these tailpipes.

The #1 tool that I recommend growers put into their grows to pay attention for new outbreaks and things of that nature are yellow sticky cards.

Some growers put them up and leave them up forever; **this is not advised.**

While sticky traps can work as a passive insecticide in that way, they are really used for monitoring infestation levels in a garden, which is why they have a grid on them.

Being able to incorporate sticky card checks, counts, and changes into your IPM regiment will give you a window into how well your processes are working.

Traps correlate with active insects in the garden; by making sure you have traps in play, you'll be able to see population increases and declines.

Root Aphid Combat

When we are combating something like root aphids, we need to make sure that we have a multi-prong approach because they're smart, fast, and multiply rapidly.

Anyone who knows me, knows I am a big advocate of the sprench application method.

The sprench comes in very handy when dealing with root aphids because they have gotten notorious for being able to outrun a drench.

If we are thinking about a dry container with a root aphid population, if you go in with a pesticide, as that moisture level seeps down into that container, the aphids are going to sense it and want to get out of the way.

The first thing to do when you are combatting root aphids is to wet your soil—run an irrigation cycle or do a partial watering—so that your container is climatized to that moisture level, then apply treatment.

This way, those root aphids are going to be less apt to outrun that moisture level once they acclimate to it.

By slowly exposing them to moisture, they are much more likely to get used to it, and therefore less likely to run away when you apply your treatments.

For example, on a Monday, say you are doing a sprench with AzaGuard.

AzaGuard's main ingredient is an antifeedant that does a few key things:

- **Removes Food Source:** AzaGuard discourages aphids from feeding on treated plant material. When it comes in contact with plant material, insects in that vicinity won't want to feed on that plant.

- **Protects Plant:** When insects don't want to chow down, we weaken them and lessen the amount of damage to plants.
- **Weakens Pests:** This combination directly affects a population's ability to be happy, healthy, and survive threats, making them easier to target.
- **Slows Reproduction:** AzaGuard impedes a pest's ability to molt (advance to the next life stage). If they can't mature properly, the population of mature insects declines, and reproduction slows.
- **Impedes Fertility:** The ovapository properties of AzaGuard affect females in the population, decreasing the hatch rates of laid eggs. If a pest is able to reproduce in spite of the above, a large portion (80%+) of those eggs will not hatch, which means a significant reduction in the insect population.

NOTE: *Make sure your treatments are making contact with your pests; if you are relying on ingestion, the efficacy goes way down. AzaGuard is a systemic chemistry; if you're going after an insect population, you need to make contact.*

While you can add AzaGuard to your nutrient schedule for prevention, a sprench approach is more effective.

Because AzaGuard is an antifeedant, if a population is present, you want to be making contact with what is there, otherwise you won't get the added benefits of growth regulation and ovapository effect.

While it can be added to your tank, it's not the best way to apply unless dealing with root-born pest like nematodes.

Azadirachtin sets you up for a weakened population of root aphids or fungus gnats, but it works best when followed with a heavy hitter like BioCeres or spinosad.

After an AzaGuard application, I recommend following up with BioCeres WP, a Beauvaria ANT-03.

The cool thing about BioCeres—*unlike many products on the market*—is that it isn't made with any petroleum, so when you put it in your root zone, it won't create a hydrophobic situation.

Plus, it utilizes larger spores (which means the chance of contact goes up) and a UV inhibitor (so it doesn't degrade as quickly when applied), both of which increase efficacy.

BioCeres works on a variety of pests, not just fungus gnats and root aphids, as you'll see throughout this chapter.

This includes white flies, canopy aphids, and a multitude of other things that are susceptible to bevaria.

Use heavy hitters like BioCeres in rotation with other effective mycoinsecticides to ensure that your pests aren't going to be developing a resistance.

Root aphids and fungus gnats can both become resistant to singular approaches, which can lead to treatment-resistant infestations (a much bigger problem).

The more you can alternate, the more you can make sure that you're mixing it up and hitting them from all different angles, the better success you will have.

Rotation is key.

Deploying immobile pesticides and barriers is key.

Staying on a program once you think you have them beat is key.

The most common issue growers face is stopping treatment because they think they got rid of a problem only to have it flare back up again.

Unless you've had a stint of months where you haven't seen pressure or infestation, it is safe to assume they are still there

Spray for 6 months after you see your last issues. After that, if don't see them, it's probably a safe bet that you've addressed it.

Best Soil Drench for Aphids:

1. **Sprench after irrigation.** Aphids run away from water after they see it. Wait 30-45 minutes so that they come back, then follow up with pesticide. You're more likely to get them when they aren't trying to evade you.

2. **Start with AzaGuard:** This affects aphid life cycle by reducing their ability to lay viable eggs, and reducing their ability to get to the adult stage.
3. **Follow up** with BioCeres, Burkholderia - Venerate, and Paleomyaces - rotate those out with microbials
4. **Rotate treatments.** In any population, there are individuals that are resistant to treatments. By rotating, that resistance isn't developed, helping to target these outliers.

Getting Gnats Out of An Indoor Container Garden:

1. Rotate AzaGuard, BioCeres, and immobile pesticide like DE
2. Make sure that you have ample dry down periods
3. Remove waste. Gnats feed off of decaying plant material: the wetter that environment is, more prolific they will become.
4. Use Azadirachtin to take away gnats' ability to grow properly. Then, use bavaria to kill them, and follow up with DE so that they can't escape.

Fungus Gnat & Root Aphid Takeaways:

1. Fungus gnats and root aphids look similar but easiest way to differentiate is wingspan size and body type.
2. When going after root aphids or fungus gnats, wet the media ahead of time and then use a sprench application to make

sure your pests are climatized to the environment so they aren't outrunning your sprays.

3. Use yellow sticky traps as monitors (not as a passive treatment). This is how you know if your efforts are working. Incorporate trap counts into your monitoring processes.
4. Diatomaceous Earth is an amazing tool for use when scouting because you can quickly dust the top of an infected plant's root zone to create an immediate barrier between pests and plants.

   Fill a cheese shaker with DE and carry it with you when you're in there doing plant work. Then, if you have an infected plant, just dust the top of it. Put down enough so it is salt and peppered (not a thick layer).
5. The more approaches we throw at them, the more success we'll have. Rotating chemistries prevents pests from developing resistance.

   Be aware that pests like root aphids can reproduce asexually, which means infestations can get out of control quickly if a mom is resistant to your treatments (which is imparted to all babies).
6. Capsicum (the "burning" ingredient in hot sauce) can also be used as it "burns" bugs. Applying this to the perimeters of saucers, tables, and rooms creates a fire line around an infestation, keeping what inside, in, and what's outside, out.
7. Sprench > Drench. BioCeres and AzaGuard can be used as soil drenches but are best used as a sprench. Drenches are not the most effective application, because root aphids in dry environments will outrun moisture, and your odds of your

treatment coming in contact go way down.

Instead, do irrigation first, then come in and do sprench (4ml/gal AG, BioCeres 9 grams/gal). Hit your canopy and the top of your media. This will allow your treatments to permeate into your containers effectively because bugs will be climatized to the moist environment and will be less apt to run away.

Hemp Russet Mites 101

Hemp Russet Mites (aculops cannabicola) are something that a lot of the industry is dealing with.

While still relatively new to the horticulture world, early studies have shown that russets cannot live on other Cannabaceae like hops, making these pests unique to cannabis and hemp.

Some growers already have good SOPs to get rid of them. If that's you, you can skip ahead.

This section is for folks that may not have encountered them yet, or folks that may still be battling mites and are looking for a solution that works.

Scouting your garden is one of the most important parts of any effective IPM routine.

Make sure you are looking for anything that is out of place and taking note when you notice damage or symptomatic plants.

What To Look For:

Russet mites live on top of your leaves and cause very distinct, visible damage.

First and foremost, you'll notice diminished growth that should tell you right away that something is not normal.

Additionally, you may notice a lackluster color.

Healthy plants typically have a sheen to them; when russets are present in a garden, that happy sheen tends to go away, leaving a matte, dull color.

And that's before russets really get established and you start to notice other symptoms developing such as edge curling/tacoing (a telltale sign of russets).

Look out for brown or yellow new growth, another telltale sign that you may have russets in your environment.

The life cycle of a russet mite is typically 21 days.

During that time, a female mite can lay 1-2 dozen eggs, having the ability to reproduce exponentially if unimpeded.

Preventative treatments start treating russets immediately by messing with their ability to feed, molt, and reproduce.

That way, even if the russets do find their way in, we are already messing with them, even before scouting them, preventing full blown infestations.

When scouting for russets, you want at least a 20-50x loupe; you can't see them with your naked eye.

You can see the damage, but won't be able to see russets themselves. Having a good loupe around your neck is going to be key.

One thing I always recommend when scouting anything in the garden is to use ziplock baggies to collect (and contain) leaves before walking out of your garden.

When I'm scouting, I pull leaves I want to look at and stick them in that bag before I walk through the rest of that space.

That way, if there is any pest pressure present, you're not just spreading it around while trying to figure out what's going on.

Putting that prophylactic in place will allow you to cleanly scope and analyze whatever plant matter that may seem

suspect because adult mites can crawl.

While mites in the larvae and nymph stage aren't very mobile, they can be spread mechanically even by a grower walking through or watering plants, and also spread easily via wind–if you have fans, mites will spread quickly.

Scouting is the key to containing and eliminating russets.

Russet Mites are definitely a pest that can be eradicated, but have to know what you're looking at.

When you start to see diminished growth, diminished tops, and that sheen has turned to a matte color with tacoing—*all signs indicative of russets***—it's time to pull out the scope and take a closer look.**

When you do look at them under a scope, russets look like maggots: they have four legs that they pull themselves around with and then a big, long, gross abdomen and thorax.

It's like something out of a horror movie.

When you see a full blown russet infestation under a scope it's pretty gross, but it's not the end of the world.

Back in the day, a lot of growers didn't know you could treat russets, and would just cut their plants down, losing countless crops.

Now, we do have options to mitigate them.

What To Use Against Russet Mites

Azadirachtin (AD): Regulates growth, take away food source, messes with mites' ability to lay eggs.

Mycoinsecticides: Product whose main ingredient(s) is(are) fungus that target pests. This includes beauvaria, paecilomyces, burkholderia, and chromobacterium, all with demonstrated degrees of efficacy against russets.

- Throwing mycoinsecticides into your rotation is definitely going to be to your advantage
- Being able to hit them from more than one angle is going to give you the success you're looking for when fighting mites.

Oils: You can also use options like mineral oil to combat russets.

Soap: Insects cannot develop a resistance to insecticidal soap, making it particularly effective against orthopod species.

Sulfur: The silver bullet for russets.

- Micronized sulfur is going to allow you to create an environment where those russets are under constant pressure, removing the conducive environment necessary for them to thrive.

- Some growers might be hesitant to use something like AD and then follow up with sulfur, which I can understand because AD is derived from Neem Oil. This is why it matters which AD product you are using.
- **Many Oil-based products will have a negative interaction with sulfur due to the extraction processes used.** Aza-Guard uses an extraction process that does not have ethanol or petroleum in it. AzaGuard's inert package is made from yucca and polysorbate (what's used in ice cream), so it's very safe, and won't give you that same negative interaction that you would see from following other oil-based products up with sulfur.

2-Step Russet SOP:

1. AD sprench on Monday
2. Sulfur spray on Friday.

———

Controlling Spider Mites in Cannabis

The Twospotted Spider Mite (informally, "Spider Mites") is a

pest that affects almost all plants.

They're a problem that has been around cannabis for a while, especially in indoor grows. If you have faced them yet, you will at some point.

While they are persistent and voracious, spider mites are definitely something that you can eliminate when you employ the proper process.

As with all pests, the first thing to do is walk your frow and look for any signs of damage.

What To Look For:

With spider mites, at first you'll see stippling-a bunch of little white dots on the tops of the leaves (it may look like your canopy was shot with rock salt).

This means that they are present in the environment and that it's time to put a procedure into place to eliminate them if you don't already have one.

In some cases, you may notice yellowing as well, as mites can take the chlorophyll out of the leaf completely, giving them a whitish color.

When you have an extreme case, you will actually get spiderwebs, which means they've been in the environment for a long period of time unaddressed.

At that point, we need to go to DEFCON-1 and immediately implement something that can hopefully save the crop.

The life cycle of spider mite can be as long as 40 days.

They start as an egg, molt into a larval stage, then they go to protonymph, then deutonymph, then to an adult. That process takes about 21-25 days on average.

Because they can live for more than a month, if you've had spider mites—even if you no longer see them—don't step off the gas.

Make sure that you are still spraying for a period of time afterwards so that you can ensure complete removal and prevent reinfestation from occurring.

This way, we are able to make the most out of our efforts and not reach a level of control only to get complacent and have to do it all again, wasting money on time and sprays.

What To Use Against Spider

Mites:

In Veg and Early Flower (up to first 3 weeks):

Azadirachtin (AD):

- Like with other pests, AD takes away mites' ability to eat, making them weak, which makes them easier to kill.
- It also screws with their ability to molt, preventing them from reaching an adult stage where they could lay eggs, and acts as an ovacide if they do lay eggs, reducing the population drastically.

Mycoinsecticides: These have also proved effective against mites, including beauvaria bassiana and paecilomyces, and burkholderia.

Oils & Soaps: You really you want to make sure you are also throwing in an oil or soap into the rotation because spider mites do have the ability to adapt to what's being thrown at them very well and they can't develop a resistance to oils or soaps.

- Oils suffocate mites, choking them out so they can't breath.
- Soaps (desiccants) suck the moisture out of their bodies, dehydrating and weakening them.
- These are an integral tool for fighting spider mites.

But, say you are in flower, and you don't want to use oils and soaps, this is where two specific predators come into play:

- Phytoseiulus Persimilis
- Californicus

These two work very well in conjunction with one another and I always recommend a live release so that you have a viable population of attacking adults in addition to hanging sachets that reinforce your predator population.

A single adult female spider mite can lay up to 100 eggs; you do the math. Sachets alone won't cut it.

By the amount of adults that could be present in a population, there's no way that a single sachet producing 3-5 predators a day is going to keep up with a female that is able to lay 100 eggs.

Simple Spider Mite SOP

Spray every 3 days for spider mites.

Eggs, when laid, take 2-4 days to hatch and become larvae. Then, the nymph stage is 2-4 days.

Spraying every 3 days hits right in the middle of each life stage, keeping up with molt cycles to target every stage of a pests' life so they aren't able to dodge what you are throwing at them.

Targeting every stage gives you the maximum efficacy.

4 Tips For Dealing with Spider Mites Like a Pro

1. Make sure you are spraying consistently but don't play "catch up."

- If you miss a day, it's not the end of the world. Don't try to do yesterday's stuff, today because then todays stuff gets pushed to tomorrow.
- Try to be as diligent as you can, especially when dealing with spider mites because consistency is going to be key with this pest.

2. Lower the temperature in the garden.

- Spider mites like hot, dry environments, so if you can lower that temperature a little bit, you are going to take away that conducive environment portion of the pyramid, which makes everything else we are doing that much more effective.
- Plus, spider mite predators like persimilis and californicus actually prefer lower temperatures, creating the right environment from them to do what they are going to do as well.

3. Employ a surfactant.

- A lot of times people will do their best to spray but will not get complete coverage.
- By employing something like an organosilicone or equivalent, you can get that surface tension coverage and be able to ensure that your spray has the adhesion you need to make contact with pests.

4. Know the rotation you are going to deploy in advance of an issue.

- This is key with spider mites because, by the time damage shows up (stippling), more often than not, you already have a serious problem on the bottom of the leaf where adults lay their eggs.
- When scouting, don't just look at the tops of your leaves; look under the bottom part and on the stems, making sure you are doing a thorough scout.
- If you are not looking at a plant in its entirety, it's not worth your time.

CHAPTER EIGHT

IPM Tactics & Implementation

Be Prepared With a Plan (So Issues Don't Become Problems)

Let's start by discussing the in's and out's of scouting and product implementation, and why those are very important steps to any IPM Process.

Two of the most important things you can do are scouting and keeping logs.

A lot of people count walking the grow as scouting because it's definitely one of the things that cannot be overlooked.

If you aren't in there walking the grow, looking through your canopy, looking for any irregularities, and constantly checking plant health, you are all but flying blind.

Scouting

Scouting is a crucial part of any integrated pest management program.

A lot of growers that I have had the pleasure of working with can tell when something isn't right, even if they don't necessarily know what they are looking for.

You don't necessarily need to be looking for a specific symptom or something that is going to be a dead giveaway to find something is wrong; scouting is just walking through your canopy.

If you see something that looks irregular, that's important.

You're in that garden (hopefully) every day, noticing those variables is going to allow you to address issues before they become issues.

With large teams, something I suggest a system for communicating and noting issues; I like irrigation flags (we'll cover more information on what to include in your scouting kit later in this chapter).

With your team, come up with a system for noting certain infestations, situations, symptoms, and treatments applied.

Markers like flags serve not only as a visual reminder to yourself that there is an issue in a quadrant in the garden, but also help quickly communicate that exact issue to the rest of the team without speaking.

I like flags because they are an obvious visual log.

In situations where you may have a dedicated IPM team or contractor who comes in at a different time than your garden tech's, having a flag system allows communication with each other and the ability to track progress.

If you see a bunch of flags, and then after treatments you see less flags, you know you are winning the battle.

Keeping Logs

A lot of growers chart nutrition and CO2 and EC and every variable you can think of but they don't track pest and pathogen pressure.

Accurate logs are very important because they allow a grower to put together a plan for the next cycle based on the current (and previous) cycle(s).

Logs allow you to draw upon your previous experience and see where you're at, what's happened, what's worked and what hasn't, and they give you a pretty good game plan for moving forward.

If for the last two years in June you have a thrip problem because it gets hot in June, and your logs show this happens every year, then you can address that ahead of time by doing preventative sprays and/or releasing some predators or other controls to mitigate the thrips when they show up as predicted.

Scouting and logs are just as important as spraying.

If you are in your garden and you're identifying certain pathogens or pests, scouting is going to allow you to have a targeted approach towards eradication of that issue.

Correctly identifying and tracking your issues is just as important as treating them with the right products.

Knowing your enemy allows you to confidently move into the next step: product implementation.

There are a ton of products out there that treat a wide range of diseases and pests that plants can encounter. Knowing what you are dealing with allows for better product implementation because you know the targets you're aiming at.

For example, let's say you had spider mites.

Zerotol probably wouldn't be the best option for you because it's not a targeted insecticide; it's used for disinfecting plants, and Sanidate 5.0 is for surfaces.

Similarly, something like a Suffoil X or DesX will be very effective against spider mites, but won't help much with mitigating powdery mildew.

Using the right products the right way will give you the most success and bang for your buck because you are putting a square peg in a square hole.

Rotation

The one thing that I really advocate with all my growers is rotating your treatments.

Even though you may have a chemistry or two that's effective against the pests that you are targeting, rotate your chemistries as much as possible because, just like anything in nature, pests and pathogens can develop resistance to what you are putting out.

Being able to have a targeted approach is good, but being able to use 4 different modes of action against that same target is going to give you much better results.

Most often, infestations get out of control because folks use the same product over and over and over, and they encourage that resistance.

While they think they are doing good and eliminating the issues, a lot of times they are actually perpetuating their problem unknowingly; populations may seem like they are in check, but a lack of rotation merely encourages a population of insects that are resistant to your efforts.

Rotating between different chemistries is going to give you the greatest amount of success possible.

And, after every rotation, make sure you're scouting for efficacy.

After treatments, you need to go through that garden and take stock of whether your efforts are working.

Count sticky cards.
Check your canopy where there were issues.
Check flagged plants.
Check for crawling mites.
See if there's still visible PM.

A proper IPM cycle comes full circle–from scouting to product implementation and back.

Scouting & Plant Work

As discussed, scouting is an integral part of any IPM strategy.

Scouting allows you to ensure that whatever you are doing is actually tailored to the situation you are dealing with.

Scouting and plant work are something you can combine on non-spray days.

If you are in the canopy doing maintenance, that's a great time to be looking at everything else in the garden and ensuring that nothing is out of place.

The 6 Things You Need In Your Scouting Kit

1. Gloves: Minimize contamination and protect yourself

2. Clean attire: Don't bring anything in with you

3. Loupe: To scope leaves

4. Plastic Baggies: For collecting samples for scoping

- Bags are for finished product right? Wrong.

  Baggies have multiple benefits. You can use bags when scouting as a prophylactic to isolate infected tissues and avoid spreading an issue throughout the garden.

For example, if you see something that looks like russet or broad mite damage, that's not a leaf you want to just pick and walk through the garden with because you're going to spread those pests to other plants and perpetuate the infection.

- I recommend removing affected leaves and putting them directly in a baggie and scoping when safely away from the rest of the garden.
- If you have ability, stick your sample bags in the fridge; if there are any insects that you need to scout for, getting them cold is going to slow them down to make them much easier to see.

5. Markers/Flags: For observation and communication

- When doing plantwork and scouting, I always stress getting yourself some of those irrigation marker flags—get different colors like orange, pink, blue, red, yellow, etc.—and come up with a system that your team is able to utilize.
- If you're in a garden doing plant work or scouting, and the red flag means spider mites, you can flag that plant without ever having to communicate with the next grower or spray operator.
- They can see, "Hey, that's a problem area so I'm going to be able to address this contamination at a later portion of the

day."

- You want to start with the cleanest areas. You don't want to spray for a problem and then go back into your clone and veg room and continue working on what you would normally be doing because you are now the vector for any infestation—disease or pathogen or pest—that occurred in another room.

- Making sure that you are flagging problem areas so other people can see them and then staying away from those areas until its go time is going to be to your benefit

6. Scissors + Solo Cup: For clean collections

- The last piece of kit that I recommend is a good pair of snips and a solo cup with either some ZeroTol at 1% or some isopropyl alcohol.

- Any time you work on a plant, make sure you disinfect your tools and your fingers before you move on to the next plant.

- That's why gloves are also essential; say you do touch a plant that is covered with an issue, and rinsing them in iso or ZeroTol isn't going to be sufficient. You can take your gloves off and move on to a new pair.

- We understand that the cost of gloves and amount of waste may make you more conservative, which is another reason to maximize the use you get out of each pair by disinfecting your fingers between plants.

Scouting ensures that the tailored approach you are using is actually working.

Regular scouting and identification ensures that you are treating the correct problems with the proper solutions. It would make no sense to treat powdery mildew with an IPM regiment of AzaGuard and BioCeres. Knowing what situation you are dealing with by scouting and make sure everybody is on the same page with markers and flags to work efficiently and effectively.

Pruning and plantwork make your sprays more effective.

If you are able to remove some of the growth that is undesirable (or not necessarily the healthiest) from under your canopy, you are not only opening up the plant to be able to get more contact and coverage when you do a spray, but you are also removing problematic tissue that could cause future issues as it decays.

Unhealthy plant material attracts pests and diseases.

Not only does pruning make sprays more effective, but it actually gives you a healthier canopy because you are removing any older growth that could be a potential vector for disease and contamination.

When scouting, make sure that you are using sticky cards, especially for any insects that fly.

If you're dealing with thrips, aphids, fungus gnats, those are all things that you want to be able to visually see a dramatic reduction in if you are monitoring with the proper tools.

By hanging sticky cards every 7 feet, you are able to visually confirm, "Hey, what we are doing is working" or "Man, that card got dirty real quick. We need to change things up."

Don't wait until you have an issue to start scouting or treating for something.

Look down the line and think about what happened last year or last run. Think, "What can I do to get out ahead of any of the problems that I may have encountered before?"

Proactive is always better than reactive.

I can't say that there's a specific chance that you won't see pests or diseases, but that chance is dramatically reduced.

If you are constantly out doing your scouting and sprays, you're going to be able to get out ahead of an infestation or an infection before it becomes a problem.

Start with your cleanest areas first.

This goes for tours as well as scouting, or any movement between grow areas.

Make sure that problem areas aren't the first room you enter. At that point, you are contaminated, and you are going to spread that contamination to whatever other part of the environment you decide to go into.

Make sure that you begin with the end in mind, and that you're not just walking into a room sight unseen hoping for the best (this is where flags come in handy).

If you see a room with a bunch of flags, and you've got rooms that don't have a bunch of flags, obviously do the flag room last.

Create a log book.

I cannot stress this enough.

By tracking run to run and year to year, you can get a sense of recurring trends and anticipate problems in advance.

If every year in May, when it gets hot, you notice the thrip population exploding, you can have procedures in place so that-when May 25th rolls around and it gets real hot-you are already prepared for that potential outbreak and you've been treating preventatively in anticipation.

Preventative methods are going to give you more success on the backend because-if you are in a preventative mode-you've got a set strategy you are adhering to.

When you get into a curative situation, that's where we throw stuff at the wall and see if it sticks, and that gets expensive, especially when crops are at stake.

At the end of the day, making sure that you know what is going on in your garden is going to be the most important part of any growers job.

The 3 Most Common Application Methods for IPM Chemistries

There 3 application methods used for most IPM tools, and the differences between them are primarily the method of dispersion, the intricacies of each method, and when each method may be beneficial.

The most basic application method that everyone is going to be familiar with is obviously a spray method.

That's going to be a blanket term for all sprays: regular sprays, fogs, electrostatic, etc.

Sprays allow you to mechanically disperse a chemistry in your environment, and, in most instances, a spray is going to be your best application method.

Sprays give you the ability to get thorough contact with every surface in the grow as well as all of the plants that could be in the environment.

There are several different applications of spraying:

- Some like to fog
- Some like to use electrostatic sprayers
- Some like backpack sprayers

Electrostatic and backpack sprayers are the best way to go.

These give you the most longevity with IPM chemistries, whereas once you get into fogging and atomization, the particulate size can actually be detrimental depending on the chemistries you're using.

Not a lot of biologicals like to be fogged or atomized because of the particulate size and pressure, which is why fogging is not always a viable application method.

In terms of a disinfection or propagation scenario, fogging can be very effective because it is going to come into contact with most of your surfaces and it's a mostly hands-off approach; you can set a fogger and let it do its thing, and then you come back after the REI and you're good to go.

Another very popular method of application that I like to recommend is called a sprench application.

I've had many growers ask me, "What is a sprench?"

A sprench is literally a hybrid of a spray and a drench; this allows you to apply your chemistry to your canopy as well as your root zone.

For example, let's say we are going after root aphids.

A sprench is a very applicable way to go about that because of that fact that you are going to address any second enstage aphid that could be in canopy as well as soil born, rhizosphere-dwelling stages -larva and nymph stages can also be addressed with that same sprench.

In a sprench application, you want to spray your canopy and hit your root ball.

Run your irrigation first, to apply "wet to wet".

Root aphids (and other pests) can outrun drenches, and by wetting your container first, you acclimate them to the moist environment so they won't be scared and try to outrun your pesticide application, which will give you a better kill rate.

The next application method you can utilize is something called chemigation.

This is a great tool if you are in flower and/or you don't want to get your calyxes wet.

A chemigation application uses your drip lines/irrigation system to apply that chemistry's benefits without having to spray.

For something like Oxiphos, you want to be using that in Weeks 3 and 6 of flower. This is also a time when calyes can be damaged by moisture from sprays or rainwater.

By using a chemigation method, you can still elicit that systemic response for 21-day period without having to get anything wet.

To recap, the 3 application methods are:

- **Spraying**
- **Sprenching**
- **Chemigation**

Tailor your approach to your situation; every situation is unique.

Understanding when and how to use your IPM processes will allow you to have a plan should an issue arise:

- You should probably sprench for root aphids, but you'll want to spray for spider mites.
- A nonionic surfactant that allows greater permeation and soaking is great when dealing with root aphids or botrytis, but terrible if you're fighting PM.

The key is making sure the chemistry you're using can get to it's target.

Part of this involves reading (and taking the time to understand) your labels.

Make sure you understand every method of application that a product gives you. There are scenarios where you might be able to use a product in ways that are more advantageous to you than a traditional spray application.

Spray Timing for Cannabis

Spray timing is a very broad term that covers duration, order, interval, time of day, and REI.

- **Duration** - How long should it take?
- **Order** - In what order should you apply your chemistry so each application is complementary?
- **Interval** - How often should you apply?
- **Time of Day** - What is the best time of day/cycle to maximize a chemistry's efficacy?
- **REI** - How can you minimize your downtime and maximize productivity?

Let's dive into each one:

Duration: How long should it take me to spray a garden?

The correct answer is: As long as it takes.

There is no quantifiable way to say whether you should be spraying for 30 minutes or 1 hour; every garden is unique, and every canopy is different. And, depending on the situation that you are in, it might take you an hour or it might even take you 3 hours.

A spray application should take as long as it takes to do it correctly.

You want to make sure that you are getting thorough coverage and that you aren't missing any spots. When you are on the attack, you want to make sure you are doing everything you can to get the efficacy out of your efforts.

Order: What order works best for spraying?

How can you best complement your last spray with your next spray, and with what you're doing each day?

What I want you to think about is, "What am I applying?"

If I'm going to be applying a growth regulant, an insecticide, possibly a fungicide like ZeroTol, what's the correct order to maximize the effectiveness of my arsenal?

The way to think about it is that every 1-2 Combo in boxing starts with a jab before coming in with the heavy hitter, so you do your jab first.

Knowing that, you're going to want to start with a tank mix of AzaGuard and Zerotol together. This ensures that you are taking away insect food sources, messing with their ability to grow and their ability to lay eggs, while also disinfesting your canopy.

Then, come in with your heavy hitter, BioCeres/Beauvaria to target those pests after the first few jabs.

If you use them in the wrong order, or you were to tank mix ZeroTol and BioCeres, they'd cancel each other out and you get no efficacy from either.

Knowing the proper order will give you the maximum benefits, and you can do this by reading your label and understanding the mode of action.

Look at the active ingredients in your products and how they work in the garden. Make sure you aren't cancelling our your efforts with your next application.

General Rule of Thumb: Don't run biologicals with or before disinfest products; disinfest then use biologicals, always.

You want to inhibit pests and pathogens, then inoculate with beneficials for the best results.

Spray Intervals: How often should you spray?

Spray intervals depend on:

- Your situation
- The product(s) you're using

Some products have a very low residual contact and efficacy in the canopy, allowing you to spray more often.

For example, something like ZeroTol is a very high level, short-lived disinfest product. Your interval for ZeroTol could be 3-5 days until a situation is controlled, or as infrequently as bi-weekly depending on maintenance needs compared to curative applications.

The severity of your situation is going to dictate your spray intervals.

Basically it comes down to what products you are going to put into play so that you can play off the chemistry itself and not cancel out one spray with another (see Spray Order).

Having the ability to do M/W/F application in a veg scenario is going to give you the best possible protection as far as covering all of your bases so that nothing finds its way into your veg. Rotate different chemistries for different days, and adhere to 7-10 day intervals for those products for the best results.

Time of Day: When should you spray?

This is one of the most common questions and I typically recommend early "morning".

I work with a lot of growers that try to spray at the end of the day. It's the last thing on the list, and they want to make sure they get it done.

But, if you think about how a pathogen like mildew grows, or if you're trying to combat PM, spraying right before the lights go off can actually be more detrimental than beneficial because we are creating a conducive environment for the mildew to grow and thrive.

If your sprays create a conducive environment, you are encouraging, not curing, your issues.

Think back to the Triangle: at the top, we have a susceptible host, followed by a conducive environment and a pest or pathogen pressure.

If all three variables are present, problems perpetuate.

If we can remove the conducive environment portion of the pyramid, we are going to make our host less susceptible and our pest or pathogen weaker.

So, if you are spraying for mold or mildew, you want to do that early in the day; as early as you possibly can.

With mold and mildew, we are trying to play off of the dry down period of the day.

It's dryer in the room during the day.

Your plants have sunlight or artificial light over them.

They're enjoying good airflow.

They're transpiring.

It's not a stagnant environment; This works to our advantage.

Conversely, at night, oftentimes some fans are cycled off, humidity can spike, and anything that thrives in a damp, dark environment has an advantage.

The worst thing we can do is spike that humidity with a boost of sprays right before the lights go off.

Any surface area that's not properly disinfested is just going to perpetuate an infection that much more. Spraying early in the day will give you a leg up and better treat mold and mildew infections properly.

And it's not just molds and mildews; I also recommend spraying early in the day for most insect-targeted chemistries.

Just like us when we wake up early in the morning, that's when insects are going to be the most active.

When they are moving around doing their thing, that's when we are going to be able to make contact with those insects, upping our efficacy and helping to solve situations.

If we spray right when lights go off, those insects are going to bed. They're in their cracks and crevices, and if you miss one, you miss them all.

The only caveat to this general rule are certain mycoinsecticides that work well in high-humidity environments.

In order for these products to maximize the longevity and efficacy, you want to hit as close to the dark cycle as possible without causing detriment to the plant so that you can play off of that humidity curve that happens when the night cycle kicks in.

That's the only scenario I would recommend applying sprays at the end of day.

If you understand the Pest-Pathogen Triangle, you also understand the reverse is true for your IPM efforts: you want the most conducive environment for your applications.

It's no longer the plant that's the susceptible host, since we are going after the insect, and now we are trying to create that conducive environment for our insecticides, further allowing you to get a leg up.

REI: Minimize Downtime & Maximize Productivity

Many growers think the best way to do this is to spray at the end of the day since lights will be off and they won't be in the room for hours.

As we discussed, nighttime is usually not the best time.

I recommend a progressive treatment routine, starting in your cleanest rooms.

Have your crews start in the cleanest environments first, treating those as needed. The cleanest environments will need maintenance applications only, and won't risk contaminating your other spaces as you move between them.

As you move from room to room, treatment intensity progresses.

Have your team do sprays as the veg crew, flower crew, etc. finishes up in each room.

Treating during the day will give you the most benefits, and if you're using products like BioSafe's, these are designed with minimal REI's in mind. Most products have 1-2 hour REI's which can allow your crew to treat the room, go to lunch, come back and be ready for action without any additional delay.

Try to coordinate your sprays to be in sync with the efforts of the rest of your crew.

What about phytotoxicity when spraying with the lights on? Won't the sprays burn?

Intense light can cause issues when spraying during the daytime, and you can avoid these by dimming or off-cycling your lights during and immediately after applications.

Turn sections of your lighting grid off while spraying.

If you're spraying three rows, turn off the lights for the first row, spray, then move on to the next, turning the first row of lights back on and off-cycling the next.

Don't spray under green lights; you will miss something.

When working in low-light and darkness, is is impossible to see and cover every potential threat. While you don't want to spray in direct light, you don't want to be spraying in the dark either.

It is to your benefit to make sure the light directly above the plant being treated is off or dimmed, but even ambient light from a few rows over is better than a headlamp or green light for identifying and addressing potential issues.

Some growers swear that you should never spray with the lights on; there's a million recipes for chili.

If you can, I recommend hanging fluorescent lights and spraying under those, as that would be better than nothing and less intense than your normal grow lights.

Capitalizing on your daytime period is the best approach you can possibly take, in my experience, because:

- It's easier to see what you're working with
- It's when pests and pathogens are most active
- It's when dry downs are naturally best for fighting issues like mildew

Spraying Cannabis in Late Flower

Spraying anything during late flower is often considered a faux pas in this industry, but it's a common question that growers have when dealing with pests and pathogens during bloom.

With that said, how and when to spray in later flower when you have to is a request that we have gotten from a couple growers, and we want to be able to cover it and clear up some of the misnomers that are out there in terms of thinking "you can't."

Because you can.

Why would you spray in late flower?

There's a variety of different reasons, but it often comes down to whether there's an issue in the garden or not.

Some type of issue in the garden is requiring those controls be put into place. At this point, any IPM effort is an effort to mitigate issues so that your harvest can be as successful as possible. Any time you are spraying in late flower, you have some type of issue.

Pathogen issues are often smaller, and treatment doesn't leave things like carcasses on the plant; You're treating spores and outbreaks with chemistries that (hopefully) break down into inert ingredients like hydrogen, oxygen, and CO2.

If you are having to spray for insects in late flower, I'm not going to chap any growers butt, but by having an issue pop up that late in flower to where that needs to be sprayed, that means that there's something else in the operation that isn't going correctly.

Try to evaluate WHY it is that you are having to spray in late flower for insects.

I would sincerely recommend reevaluating your strategies and SOPs if you are having pronounced insect issues in the final phases of your flower cycle.

Now, shit does happen, and there are some times where you've got more shit than shovel, and you're just trying to get caught up and things find their way in.

If you're spraying for bugs in late flower, there's something wrong in the workflow, so start there.

On the other hand, if you have to spray in late flower for a pathogen or mold outbreak in the garden, that's not necessarily a sign of a workflow issue, as pathogens can propagate quickly and can be exacerbated by unexpected things happening.

Equipment failures like an A/C failing, dehumidifiers failing, or even the power going out and you not being able to have a day cycle can all contribute to pathogen pressure.

If you are going into this diligently, you're doing everything that you can do ahead of time to ensure that your run is going to be as clean as possible, and something like an air conditioner throws you a curveball in Week 8, applying the right sprays with the right chemistries can help you have as much success as you possibly can without sacrificing the entire crop.

When problems in late flower occur, most growers don't have a game plan; they don't know what to do, and they've been told by all their friends not to ever spray anything, even if it means saving their harvest.

Some growers will just tell you to let it ride.

Some growers will tell you to chop it down.

In reality, what we need to do is make sure you have a solid SOP for when the crap hits the fan and you are caught in that situation where you don't have a choice and you have to spray it.

By understanding the chemistries that you are applying—as far as residuals, efficacy, and inhibition qualities—you are going to be able to make sure that any sprays you apply are going to be that much more effective.

Let's talk about HOW to spray in late flower.

There's a few different ways to go about it:

- Backpack sprayers
- Dram sprayers
- Foggers

The best way that I have found to do late flower pathogen mitigation is to be able to utilize a sprayer with a medium to large droplet size in addition to a PAA chemistry like ZeroTol and a nonionic surfactant, such as Natural Wet, Coco Wet, or Thermax 70; there's a bunch of different ones out there.

What you are trying to do is get that permeation effect from the nonionic surfactant to be able to soak into that cola.

Something like botrytis grows from the inside out.

Unless you are very diligent in your scouting, you often won't know you have botrytis until you know you have botrytis.

Doing sprays as a preventative with that 1% solution of ZeroTol mixed with that nonionic surfactant is going to ensure that you are going to saturate all the way down to the stem and eradicate any of those spores that could be there.

The reason that we use a chemistry like ZeroTol over something like possibly a copper or neem derivative fungicide is because ZeroTol breaks down into oxygen, water, and carbon dioxide.

In an environment where any contaminants matter, you aren't introducing anything foreign that could ever cause your product to fail testing or really degrade the potency or affect your terpene profiles because your sprays break down into inert compounds.

Zac's 3-Point Combo:

- Medium-to-Large Droplet size Sprayer
- ZeroTol 2.0
- Nonionic surfactant (to cover gamut of pathogens)

The idea is to spray BEFORE you cut down.

Cannabis is very similar to a rose in terms of osmotic pressure needing to be present and that turgidity needing to be there to withstand environmental stresses.

Sprays are a form of environmental stress.

We try to mitigate stress as much as possible, but even rain water can damage calyxes.

When we are spraying, not only are we trying to disinfest the crop thoroughly, but we are trying to cause the least amount of damage we possibly can.

That's why I recommend spraying before you cut down if microbial testing is a concern in your state because you are able to utilize a chemistry such as ZeroTol that is going to allow you to be very discriminating against yeast, mold, and fungi, while still having the ability to break down into completely inert ingredients that are going to be found in the environment anyways.

By doing so, you are adhering to any other farmers' standards:

If you were growing cucumbers…
If you were growing tomatoes…
If you were growing potatoes…

…you would have to have a disinfection phase in between your growth and the market.

About a decade ago, there was actually a case here in Colorado and these guys were cantaloupe growers who ended up in jail because they didn't disinfect.

The growers weren't trying to do anything malicious but their disinfesting unit broke.

And some people got some lysteria from their product.

And those people died.

And one of those growers is still in Cañon City Prison to this day because of that oversight in judgment.

So, I'm imploring you to please try to adhere to some food

safety standards moving forward because everything we grow is either smoked, eaten, or rubbed on somebody's skin.

Food safety requirements are coming soon; be prepared for that and know that what you are doing is not only ethical, it's a standard in all other parts of agriculture.

For late flower sprays, use lighter chemistries so you won't have any residual carryover into your final product, especially if you are making extracts or edibles.

PAA + H2O2 is a great way to sterilize the canopy (aka ZeroTol).

Say we are in Week 7 or Week 8, we still have a ways to get to the finish line and we have some issues, what should we do?

I recommend applying something like ZeroTol and then following up with something that has a citric acid active ingredient for a couple reasons:

- **Citric acid is a mold inhibitor.** If you can disinfest and then inhibit, you'll get better longevity out of both products.

- **Citric acid is also a preservative used in food products** all the time, so we know it is safe for human consumption to a degree.

  By utilizing something like citric acid over something like garlic oil, or something that is going to leave residuals on the plant, you are able to get into that later flower stage, have less detriment to your final product, and still harvest the best crop possible.

Citric acid might get you 5-7 days out of an application, prolonging that spray window so that, again, we are not causing extra environmental stress to those plants by applying more than we need to.

Obviously, the goal of this is to be able to pass microbial testing; to be able to have clean medicine and recreational products for the general public and to be able to learn something so that we don't keep replicating these issues.

And I know most growers are going to say "I never spray anything in late flower," *but sometimes you have to.*

You can't get to the point of harvest and then do something unethical like put out contaminated product.

This is a guideline for folks moving forward so that you can have the knowledge and know that what you are applying to this product is going to have the least effect on the end user and you are doing it as ethically as possible.

Zac's Late Spray SOP:

Using Zerotol in those final stages is a great way to disinfest your products for microbial testing.

It is designed for spoilage diseases and preservation of your products, so you are within the label language to use it as such.

Utilizing an inhibitor like citric acid is definitely going to be to your benefit if you've got a longer period to go. Just be aware of your environment and the pest-pathogen triangle

In order for that triangle to exist, you need to have a pest, a susceptible host, and you need to have a conducive environment.

If you can eliminate any one of those points on the triangle, it's not going to be stable and it cannot exist.

So if you find yourself having to spray over and over and over again in late flower because you always get botrytis, it might be time to maybe look at your HVAC system again and make sure that you've got proper dehumidification and proper controls.

If you've got Powdery Mildew that shows up same time every time in certain strains and you're already utilizing OxiPhos, ZeroTol and an inhibitor, it's time to look at what other aspects are in that grow (I.e. that conducive environment part of that pyramid) and address those because pests and disease cannot exist unless we give them the right environment to do so.

If you have Powdery Mildew (PM) in late flower:

- **Use an OxiPhos rotation** and get in on that as early in the plant stage as possible to elicit that induced systemic reaction (ISR). This will mitigate the hyphae from PM so that it doesn't become a recurring issue

- **Physically, get in there** and try to prune the plants up as much as you can because desiccation will help with PM.
- **Try to stop temp and humidity swings.** Even if it is cold and humid all the time, that's better than going humid-dry-humid-dry-humid or cold-hot-cold-hot. Try to stablize that as much as possible.

Pre & Post-Harvest Disinfesting For Your Facility and Canopy

In the facility and in the garden, there are certain things you can do as a grower to minimize the chances of having issues later on.

By focusing on being preventative rather than curative, you can ensure that your efforts are going to be above board as much as possible and result in the least amount of issues possible.

Pre-Harvest Disinfesting

Pre-harvest disinfesting in a facility consists of making sure that you have a protocol in place where your environment is being disinfested periodically.

There are different tools for growers to be able to achieve this, my personal favorites are the **BioFoamer** and the **BioMats**:

- A BioFoamer allows you to target specific areas for disinfesting without worrying about any type of drift or overspray that could get on your crop so you can thoroughly disinfest a grow during process.
- BioMats help to ensure you and your team aren't tracking any sources of contamination in on the undersoles of your shoes.

Making sure you are starting clean and staying clean is key to your success.

ZeroTol and Sanidate are great tools for sterilizing your environment during the growing process; fog, foam, or spray, they are all going to help give you that same means to an end.

In terms of disinfesting your crop itself:

Zac is a proponent of spraying the plants before they come down with Zerotol 2.0.

ZT is a high level but short-lived disinfest product that can be utilized in a way where you are addressing any microbial (yeast, mold, fungi) concerns before you ever cut the plant down

In general, it's a good agricultural practice, and a standard food safety practice, to sterilize a crop before it goes out to market.

By utilizing an applicator the day before or the day of harvest, you're going to have your trim team be able to cut down the most disinfested crop possible. And, by doing so, you are adhering to the same standards that a cantaloupe grower or a tomato grower or a potato grower would have to have in place.

2 Main Reasons to Spray BEFORE You Chop:

1. First and foremost, you can't be accused by your regulatory department of trying to cheat your sample tests because you subjected the entire crop to the same process.
2. The other main advantage to spraying before you cut down (rather than a post harvest dunk) is maintaining osmotic pressure. Cannabis is a lot like a rose in terms of osmotic pressure; you're going to see the least detriment to your flavor and terpene profile when the plant has the most osmotic pressure (aka before chop). If you can spray it while the plant is still attached to the stalk, you're going to minimize the impact of those sprays.

I have tons of growers in the U.S. that do these pre-chop sprays, and I challenge consumers to tell me which buds have been sprayed; I haven't met someone who can tell which crops were treated and which weren't.

Because, if you are using a chemistry like ZeroTol that breaks down into oxygen and water, you are kicking out an ethical, safe product with no residuals.

Especially in medical markets, if you sell something contaminated to someone with a compromised immune system, that would be a very sad day to make someone sick because of the medicine they were choosing to use.

For those that prefer not to spray, you can do a post-harvest disinfection dunk/dip with ZT, but it's not the preferred method for 2 reasons:

1. **While it is an effective way to address microbials like yeast, mold, and fungi, it's not my favorite way to do it because of loss of osmotic pressure.**

   If you do have any detriment to your flavor, terpene profile, or potency, it's going to happen after the chop from a dip rather than while you were applying something to a live plant.

2. **The other big downside to a dip is you are basically degradation that solution every time you are sticking something in there and disinfesting it, so each dip is less effective than the one that preceded it.**

   If you are doing dunks, the main way to address the concern of degrading chemistries (and the efficacy of your efforts) is to regularly test the solution throughout the process. Invest in some LaMotte PAA test strips, and basically test your solution every dozen or so plants, to see where your peroxide and PAA levels are, and then add to the tank as needed. But this is not my preferred method.

When disinfecting a crop, if you can spray ahead of time, you're going to be doing yourself a favor.

Remember, there's a 1 hour reentry interval (REI) for ZeroTol in an indoor environment.

So, you could have your applicator show up, spray at 8AM, and as long as he's done by 9AM, you can have your trimmers show up at 10AM to cut down that disinfested crop and not even skip a beat.

Post-Harvest Facility & Equipment Disinfesting

For your post-harvest disinfesting efforts, utilizing something like Sanidate 5.0 whenever possible will ensure that you get that food safety level of disinfesting.

While food safety standards are not mandated in the industry yet, it's only a matter of time.

And with everything going on in the world, when you utilize something like Sanidate, you're going to have a zero-rinse chemistry that specifically targets things like e. coli, lysteria, and salmonella, all standard requirements by the FDA for food safety claims.

Zero-rinse chemistries like ZeroTol and Sanidate allow you to have the highest level of disinfesting possible while breaking down into oxygen and water.

Sanidate can be applied for 5-10 minutes at a rate of 1 fl. Oz. per gallon to kill all listed pathogens. It is one of the highest level disinfectants that you can employ without negatively impacting the environment.

When you are doing that post-harvest disinfesting, make sure you are addressing all aspects of the grow, including irrigation:

- Take your drippers and soak them in Sanidate.
- Scrub your main lines with Green Clean Acid Cleaner and then follow up with Sanidate to get rid of any bio-burden so you don't have pathogen issues next time
- Go through and foam everything in the grow so that every hard surface is disinfected
- And then, possibly employ something like Gard'nClean or ProKure packets to prolong your disinfesting window

Remember, understanding your chemistries is important if you want them to work.

For example, ZeroTol & Sanidate don't kill bugs. They are not labeled as insecticides. But that doesn't mean growers don't mistakenly try to use them to treat bugs.

Refer to the chapters on common pests for recommendations on how best to eradicate pest populations. An integral part of keeping a garden clean is preventing and addressing insects.

Plant & Facility Disinfesting for Healthy Crops

What is Disinfesting?

Disinfesting is the act of cleaning and removing residual threats from tools, equipment, and facilities to prevent future spread.

Disinfesting is one of the most important steps in growing.

Most growers know this and want to do it well. Unfortunately, they have all too often been left ill-equipped to do so because they have not been given the proper tools (or authority) to be able to take their efforts to that next level of cleanliness.

Why is Disinfesting Important?

If you are not cleaning your environment properly, it is going to be a breeding ground for things like pests and disease.

Disinfesting processes are just as important as watering your plants or making sure your lights are on.

3 Application Methods For Disinfesting Your Space

There are 3 primary ways to disinfest an environment:

- Foaming
- Fogging
- Mop & Rags

My personal favorite is to use foaming applications.

Foaming allows you to make sure that your applications are sticking to your surfaces. It makes sure that you are getting the contact time you need to disinfest properly, and it's a zero-rinse application so there's no additional clean-up work.

A lot of folks also use foggers for disinfesting.

Foggers are a great tool for use in-between runs because you can kind of set it and forget it.

You can even do them when you're not there and the fogger can be set on a timer and just go. But, if you aren't foaming, fogging is definitely another really good way to do it.

Then, there's the old school way to do it with a mop and rags.

Each of these methods will allow you to achieve a desirable level of disinfesting, though some will be better suited for your specific needs.

However you get there doesn't really matter as long as you're disinfesting.

Plant Disinfesting

Plant disinfesting is essential because of the fact that if we allow pathogens or disease to propagate in our garden we are not going to have a successful yield.

We need to make sure that we are employing the right products at the right time so that we can disinfest things so that we produce a safe product that passes testing.

We prefer ZeroTol for plant disinfesting in cannabis.

Both ZeroTol 2.0 and ZeroTol HC contain high levels of PAA. ZeroTol's chemistries allow you to maintain a very high level of disinfesting throughout the entire process.

And, as we've mentioned, there's zero residuals after application, so you won't have to worry about rinsing anything off as it breaks down into oxygen and water.

4 Reasons To Disinfest Your Plants

1. Allows you to have a successful harvest

2. Mitigates issues that you could unknowingly have throughout the process
3. Gives you a better overall product
4. Gets you more money for that product

If you have a dirty product, it's not going to sell for top dollar; disinfesting goes hand in hand with product value.

On top of product value, testing is a big thing commercial growers have to deal with.

By disinfesting your plants properly, you can ensure that when it comes time to sell your product, it adheres to all standards set forth for the industry.

PLANT DINSINFESTING APPLICATION RATES: ZeroTol 2.0 and ZeroTol HC

- **Pre-harvest Disinfesting**: 1% (1:100; 37ml/gal)
- **Preventative Disinfesting**: 0.4% (1:256; 15ml/gal) applied every 5-7 days to ensure disinfesting throughout entire process

Disinfesting The Grow Itself: Hard Surfaces

Backing up a step further, all hard surfaces along the way to the grow need attention, not just those in the grow.

Hard surfaces in the grow itself, but also your office, your car, your phone—make sure that you have processes and products in place to keep things as clean as possible throughout not just the growing process but everything else that you do.

If you start clean, and stay clean, it's going to give you a better end result.

For hard surface disinfesting, we really like Sanidate 5.0, Sanidate APD (all purpose disinfectant) and Sanidate wipes.

The APD and wipes are awesome for offices, vehicles, and common areas because of the fact that you still have that very high level of disinfection that you would use in your garden but it's safe and easy to apply to your hard surfaces in your daily life.

By keeping your daily life clean, you're going to lessen the potential of being a vector for contamination.

If you're going from one garden or room to another, or you're sitting in an environment that's less than clean, when you come back, you can make sure you (and anything you touched) are as clean as possible.

We recommend using Sanidate for grow disinfesting.

It can be applied basically anywhere that is going to be a high value area, not necessarily office building. That includes grows, cure areas, reservoirs, as well as processing rooms and tools.

SD5 allows you to have the highest level of disinfesting, gets you that food safety claim, and makes sure to address things like e. coli, salmonella and listeria (It's also labeled for human coronavirus as well).

APPLICATION RATES: Sanidate 5.0

For all growing surfaces: 1:100 or 37ml/gallon.

Cleanliness is Next to Godliness

The importance of disinfesting your hard surfaces is just as important as disinfesting your plants.

By doing so, you are able to claim certifications like Food Safety that allow growers to set themselves apart.

Food Safety Standards are not mandated in cannabis yet, but the authors of this book believe that it is not a question of if it is coming, but when.

With everything else that's been going on in the world recently, cleanliness is on everyone's mind.

Having a procedure in place to adhere to those standards now is going to allow you to be ahead of the curve when they make it mandatory down the line. If we wait until it's a mandatory thing, that's when things get expensive for everyone.

Be proactive: think about what's going to happen in 6 months or a year, and plan for it.

Not just in your disinfesting, but also in how you approach your entire operation.

That way, we are not caught with our hands in our pockets when things change and things like Food Safety become a requirement.

Proactive vs. reactive, just like IPM.

CHAPTER NINE

High Quality H2O

Water 101, Treatment, & Analysis

When it comes to growing, if your water source is contaminated, you're fighting an uphill battle from the start.

Knowing what makes your water high quality—as well as how to treat common water-borne issues that can decimate harvests in late flower—is key to ensuring your grows will have the best chance of producing the highest quality crops.

Water 101 in Cannabis

Two of the most common questions surrounding water and IPM are:

1. How do IPM chemistries interact with certain water qualities?
2. How do these chemistries keep grows clean on every level?

Chain of Custody

For starters, your water has to come from somewhere.

That could be an irrigation pond, a well, or a municipal source; some initial place where your water is coming from.

The first step is to test your source water.

For larger commercial growers, there are a variety of testing options, including businesses like BioSafe that will test for negative pathogens and bacteria, and offer suggestions for remedies. Ask your IPM supplier if they offer this service.

The next step in the water chain of custody is some type of filtration.

Some people can get away with just using regular old tap water, but the majority of us do not have that luxury.

After your source water, the second step is filtration.

Some growers use RO water. Other growers just use a carbon sediment filter.

Zac The Grow Guy's Take: A carbon sediment filter is more than sufficient for what we are trying to do.

RO is actually overkill, especially if we are going to try to treat any pathogens that may be present in this water column. And I never recommend combining plain RO water with a PAA chemistry (sterilizing agent in products like ZeroTol 2.0).

RO is dead water (bicarbonate content has been removed).

Bicarbonate content offsets acidic components that could be in that water column.

If we are treating water with PAA, we add PAA to a water column with 0 buffer whose pH has already dropped through oxidation. RO water comes out of the machine at 7.0.

After 24 hours, it's going to be at a pH of ~5.5 just from being exposed to the regular environment. Mix that pH 5.5 with an acid that doesn't have any type of compensator in it and you're looking at a ph of probably around 3.0.

If you then use potassium hydroxide (pH UP) without the interaction of the bicarbonate content, you are mixing an acid and a base, basically neutralizing and rendering both products ineffective.

Zac's filtration of choice is a KDF 85, sufficient for 95% of water sources.

If you are in a situation that your well water is severely contaminated and you don't even want to spike your RO with it a little bit to add bicarbonate, you can add weak strength base NPK feed until you reach 0.3 EC so you don't see that pH drop.

This is also how we recommend building your buffer if you are doing direct injection for disinfesting; I always recommend fertilizer first so that we have the ability to offset that pH drop from the PAA.

After figuring out your filtration of choice, the next step in the chain is irrigation.

How you inject fertilizer and disinfest products—using injector skids or just dosing tanks out—will dictate how you apply water treatments.

We recommend running your fertilizer first, then disinfesting using a PAA chemistry like Zerotol 2.0.

If you are using your chemistry in a reservoir situation, use something like LaMotte PAA strips to test your reservoir in real time and see where your level of PAA is in correlation with water treatment level (typically shoot for 5-7ppm of PAA).

Then, you can dial your rates up or down accordingly so that you are right in that sweet spot with enough to kill any bacteria there while not having any residual that could cause ill effects.

After fertilizer and disinfesting, the water goes to your

plants.

When you are going to be treating your water, 5-7 PPM of PAA is safe for constant rate but high enough to kill bacteria, algae, and zoo spore. This cleans the water before it gets to the plants, lessening chance of infection by keeping irrigation lines clean.

An added benefit of treating your water is that you'll have a cleaner irrigation system, too.

When bioburden and mineral scale are unable to accumulate, yoru entire system functions more efficiently.

PAA (Zerotol 2.0) Direct Injection Rates:

- 1:3000-1:5000
- Utilize PAA strips to see how much comes through system

Sanidate 5.0 Direct Injection Rates

- For situations using more than 6500 gallons a day
- 1:7,000- 1:10,000

Both ZeroTol and Sanidate can be used while plants are in the garden.

2-Step Water System Treatment

In between runs, it is a best practice to do line shocks and flushes.

1. Roughen up any bioburden or mineral scale that could have accumulated during the run. We recommend using 1% Green Clean Acid Cleaner in your system for 1-2 hours. This works like sandpaper to expose and break up accumulations.
2. Once you've created this rough surface area in your system, follow up with a disinfest product (Sanidate 5.0) solution and soak overnight.

Step one creates cracks and crevices in buildup, and step two comes in to clean up the mess.

This 2-Step process will ensure your system is as close to brand new as possible, making sure you make the most of your inputs.

To get system as sterile as possible, always make sure to run at least 2x the amount of clear water the system can hold as your final flush before reassembly.

Example:

1. Step 1: Green Cleaner.
2. Step 2: Sanidate

3. Step 3: Flush. Then, plug everything back in and run your double-volume amount of water. *(For a 5-gal system, put 10 gallons of water through it to make sure no there's no residual funkiness or disinfest product left in system.)*

A Note on Ponds and Irrigation Ditches

If you are using a pond or irrigation ditch as source water, you can treat the source as well.

Sodium precarbonate (found in products like Green Cleaner Pro) is an awesome option for algae and fungal spores that could be propagating in your irrigation pond.

One of the biggest issues with irrigation ponds is that, more often than not, the water is stagnant. Utilizing a chemistry that will put oxygen into the environment while at the same time killing any negative pathogens is going to be to your benefit.

We recommend treating outdoor source water and irrigation ponds with Green Clean Pro and Pondblock.

Water Treatment & Analysis: When & Why

For the longest time, water-borne pathogens have been something that the industry has dealt with but not necessarily recognized.

When You Should Be Doing Water Analysis

Routine tests are very important as a grower in any facility.

Knowing your pathogen content as well as the water profile is going to allow you to make educated decisions on what you should be doing moving forward, so routine tests are clutch.

Quarterly tests are best.

If you can't get quarterly test done, testing annually is essential. At least do it once a year so that you know if anything has changed or if there is a pathogen load in the water column that needs to be addressed.

The best thing about water analysis is that it gives us real-time data on both pathogen and disease pressure loads so we know exactly what we are dealing with.

This gives us an educated approach that is more likely to solve these issues efficiently, rather than just throwing stuff at the wall and seeing what sticks.

Water tests are your best friend, especially if you are growing in DWC or rockwool (inert media). In these situations, it is important that you make sure that your water is as clean as you can possibly get it.

If things are normal and then all of a sudden you notice some diminished growth or odd growth patterns, it's test time.

If the nutrient profile has not changed, and the media has stayed consistent, but something else is off, more often than not it's the water column. Even if your source water is filtered, that doesn't mean that it is totally clean.

When You Should Be Doing Water Treatment

After you get your water test, you want to start out with line shocks as close to your input source as you can possibly get.

You want to shock your lines so that—if there is any pathogen or disease pressure present in your water column or any biomass that could be in the lines themselves—we aren't just harboring microbes to perpetuate the infections.

Line Shock SOP:

1. GreenClean Acid Cleaner
2. Followed by Sanidate 5.0
3. Then, institute water treatment to clean the system and keep it clean

Treating with H2O2 and PAA (ZeroTol) is actually more effective than treating with chlorine because we can actually go after dormant fungal spores, and chlorine is not going to touch that.

A lot of people ask me, "What's the difference between this popular product containing HPA and SaniDate and ZeroTol?"

The primary difference is efficacy and inert breakdown into oxygen and water.

Many products on the market break down into salts that are not necessarily beneficial for all systems.

Direct injection is going to be better than mixing batch tanks because you are getting the freshest product possible into the lines to ensure maximum amount of disinfesting.

If you have to do batch tanks, it's not end of world, just make sure you add your ZeroTol last.

1. Nutrients first.
2. Then ZeroTol or Sanidate (uses the bicarbonate content to avoid a pH drop with plain RO water)

Why Water Treatment is important

Water testing and treatment protects crops from pathogens that can easily be mitigated.

Start clean so you can stay clean, and it all starts with water.

Making sure you know exactly what is in your water column and planning accordingly will allow you to tailor an approach that avoids issues that start at the source. It will also make sure things like pythium never find their way to the plant by oxidizing spores early in the chain of custody.

Once you have identified and disinfested, stay clean with

140

maintenance rate water treatments to ensure nothing sneaks into your grow.

Maintenance treatment rates will have negligible effect on established bacillus and other beneficial microbial populations. These lower rates do the job of keeping the water clean without having to worry about killing off all of your beneficials.

Water Q&A

How much does it cost to test your water?

Tests often cost $0-250+ depending on what your needs are and the lab you're using for testing.

For example, some manufacturers will offer water testing if you are a large commercial customer or do a certain amount of business with them every year.

Resources for water testing for home growers?

If you're a smaller scale grower, we recommend finding a local Pool & Spa store.

These stores typically offer a low cost basic water analysis that will get you a little more clarity before you invest in a more advanced test.

SOPs You Can Use Immediately

With all of the information included in this book, you're better prepared than most growers to prevent and address any issues that may pop up in your facility.

To help make all of this actionable, below you'll find two specific SOPs that you can save, print, and use in your efforts to ensure a high level of success, compliance, and quality.

The following 7 SOPs are meant to be a guide for you, but are not written in stone! Feel free to adjust as needed to fit your specific needs.

- **Chapter 10:** Full-Cycle Cannabis Cultivation SOP
- **Chapter 11:** Mother Plant Care SOP
- **Chapter 12:** Propagation & Cloning SOPs
- **Chapter 13:** IPM & Plant Care Workflow Calendar
- **Chapter 14:** Bringing in New Genetics SOP

143

CHAPTER TEN

Full-Cycle Cannabis Cultivation SOP

From Start to Finish: IPM SOP For The Cannabis Grower

When Zac joined the team over at BioSafe, one of the projects he helped drive was the creation of the Cannabis Crop Production Program.

By putting this together, the team was able to design an SOP that staggered products in a certain way so that they are they most effective while allowing you to achieve your goals with the least amount of expense and the greatest amount of efficacy possible.

As we all have experienced, there are issues that can pop up in any phase of growing, so this SOP is going to allow you to be able to address any situations that you may encounter and have a solid game plan for those situations.

This section gets deep in the weeds, but it's all summarized in Chapter 13 in a clean chart and calendar that you can print out and stick up in your grow for quick reference.

It all starts in propagation

So, the first thing that I recommend to any grower is to treat your mother plants before you ever take your clones or cuttings. *(More on this in Chapters 11 & 12)*

If you can have clean moms, cloning is going to stress out your cuttings less and give you better, more viable clones that are ready to go.

There are a few different products that people will use to treat their mother plants, but one of my favorite combinations for hemp or cannabis is a Zerotol and OxiPhos spray together at 1:300 of each.

By treating with OxiPhos and ZeroTol, you're getting a very high disinfectant rate that also elicits ISR.

That gives you about 21 days of residual protection against certain pathogens and bacteria that could be present or targeting those clones.

That 21-day residual is also going to help anyone that sells clones as we've mentioned, because of the fact that you are going to ensure that it is going to be the healthiest cutting possible by the time it gets to your end customer.

Then, we throw that ZeroTol in there just to make sure we are disinfecting everything from the jump.

Typically, I recommend doing a cutting dip with ZeroTol at a 1:256 ratio (15 ml/gallon of water) when you take your clones.

But, instead of dunking one clone at a time, it's advantageous to be able to dunk as many cuttings as possible, simultaneously.

To do that fill up a big tub (like one of those cement mixing tubs that they sell at the hardware store) and get yourself like a piece of window screen and get your solo cups full of 40-50 cuttings, and lay them out across the window screen, and dunk all at once for 45-60 seconds.

Then, you can submerge 40-50 clones at a time. Within that 45-60 seconds, you will have exponentially increased productivity by being able to treat them all at once. Plus, you minimize the impact of diluting that dunking reservoir over time by doing one dunk, all at once.

The other thing ZeroTol is good for with cuttings is addressing any issues within your domes or aerocloners.

ZeroTol (at a 1:256 or 15ml/gal rate) is a safe foliar spray to help mitigate any white mold or botrytis looking stuff that could be growing in the domes due to high humidity.

Once you have established your root zone, we recommend using a microbial inoculant like TerraGrow.

CAUTION: You do not want to use ZeroTol and TerraGrow together in the same applications/solution; ZeroTol will neutralize your TerraGrow.

Anybody that has heard Zac talk about IPM knows that he's a proponent of cleaning the slate ahead of time (an ounce of prevention is worth a pound of cure, as they say).

If you can use the ZeroTol the day before you apply your TG, you're going to make sure that that media is sterilized.

That clean slate is going to allow much better colonization of all the things in your microbial inoculants—like bacillus subtilis, pumilus, megaterium and licheniformis.

TerraGrow Transplant Slurry

We recommend using TerraGrow during stressful situations like transplanting to boost plant health and encourage growth.

Because it is a biostimulant that contains both kelp and humic acid, it encourages nutrient absorption and acts as a natural growth enhancer that minimizes stress.

When transplanting, you can also use TerraGrow (3oz/10 gal) to make a slurry solution for dunking your root ball in.

This is the best approach to go for transplant inoculation to minimize stress and shock that can delay your timeline.

Mix that slurry solution up, and then, as you are doing your transplants, dunk that root ball into that very high rate of active microbial. Then, once you've established those populations, that's when you begin to follow up with a bi-weekly application of TerraGrow (0.5-1.0 grams/gallon depending on media type).

Veg Phase

Once we have actually gotten into the growth phase, the vegetative phase, we can begin to utilize sprays, sprenches, and root drenches periodically and proactively.

We are big proponents of spraying in veg whether you see a problem or not.

Because veg is the smallest footprint with the most allowable control as far as overall space that you can have the greatest amount of tools at your disposal, it's advantageous to prevent issues here before you head into flower.

Even though some flower rooms might be smaller in terms of square footage, the amount of pesticides that you are allowed to use in a flowering phase may not be on par with what you actually need to do to address certain situations, pests, and pathogens.

Getting on a treatment rotation in veg—treating M/W/F or T/Th/Sat or whatever works for you— is going to allow you to have the most effective system.

Here's why: You want to think about your IPM approaches like a boxing combo, almost like a jab and a 1-2 combo.

"Will pests get used to this though?"

That rotation of different products is key in any IPM approach because we don't want pests to get comfy or develop a resistance.

With that said, things like OxiPhos and ZeroTol are not being targeted towards insects, so pests can't really get used to their applications.

In terms of Azadirachtin, there's never been any mutational resistance ever documented that shows that pests can get used to it. So, as long as you are using it in a proactive and ethical way, they should not develop that resistance.

Most often, insects develop resistance to things when people use them off-label and don't realize that if 10 ml didn't do it, 20 ml probably isn't going to either.

MONDAY: Azadirachtin *(AzaGuard's main ingredient)*

Azadirachtin is key for the rest of your applications; it makes sure that everything else you are doing is actually effective.

First and foremost, make sure that the product you are using is free of contaminants like ethanol or petroleum, or any secondary metabolites that could leave behind residuals and cause unintended results.

If you put ethanol in your root zone or on flowers that are resinous, you're applying a solvent to those resins. Ethanol is a solvent, so you could be degrading your potency or hurting your crop by exacerbating certain conditions with said solvent.

Azadirachtin is an antifeedant. When we start out with azadirachtin, we are taking away an insect's food source. If they are unable to eat, they are going to be easier to kill, that's why that is such an important step.

Products like Azaguard also have ~90 different limonoids in the formulation in addition to azadirachtin to help with repellency and ovipository qualities, and, to a degree, growth regulation.

If we can keep the target population from molting properly with that growth regulation capability, they can't get to an adult phase, which means you're dealing with much less of an infestation that subsequent week because of the fact that getting to that mature stage is not an easy task for them once they have been exposed to azadirachtin.

AzaGuard is also an ovacide. If your pests lay 10 eggs, but only 1 hatches, that's 90% less of an infestation that you're dealing with that subsequent week

For these reasons, we recommend starting out with azadirachtin to make sure that anything else you are putting out is going to be that much more effective.

Monday Recap: First week of Veg, AG + ZT+OP together

- Cleans everything up (ZT)
- Takes away pest food sources (AG)
- Elicits ISR (OP)

Tuesdays: Cloning & Plant Work

Use Tuesdays for tasks like defoliation, scouting, replacing sticky cards, and placing flags as needed.

As we've discussed, one thing we recommend for a lot of growers is to get some irrigation marker flags from the hardware store and come up with a system with your team where those colors correlate to what's going on in the garden.

For example, say the Blue flag means there's powdery mildew.

You're out in the grow taking clones and doing your scouting, and you see a plant that could be affected, stick a blue flag in it. On Wednesday, when you're going through and applying your chemistries, you gave yourself a heads up into what's going on in the garden.

Zac has run a lot of large scale operations and it's common to tell yourself, "Oh, I'll remember it was the 5th plant in the 6th row" and then you get back in there the next day and you have no idea which plant it was because you have so many other things you have to be able to accomplish.

Systems like irrigation markers are clutch so that you can communicate with team members without even having to speak to one another, and avoid the perils of misremembering which plants are affected.

Tuesday Recap: Cloning & Plant Work

- Taking cuts
- Scouting
- Marking

Wednesdays: Heavy-Hitter Rotation

To continue the comparison, this is where your uppercuts start to come into play after you've disoriented with your jabs and combos.

Remember:

- Monday's, we weaken them
- Tuesday's, we scout them
- Wednesdays, we hit 'em where it hurts

Those heavy-hitters are going to be your products that are going to be mycoinsecticides and pesticides that are EPA-registered and safe to use on cannabis products (not ornamentals).

BioSafe recommends using BioCeres for soft-bodied insects as a preventative approach.

There are also other mycoinsecticides that depending on your type and level of infestation may be advantageous to rotate with the BioCeres. Ben likes to employ pyrethrin in his rotation, for example.

There are some newer products on the market that are bio-based and very effective, and Zac always recommends keeping up with the latest and greatest research and chemistries.

Pay attention to what other markets are approving (or unapproving).

Keeping tabs on what new approved products are coming out will help you stay up-to-date on what is working, as well as what doesn't seem to be effective anymore.

In the traditional horticulture world, there are a lot of people that put a lot of knowledge out there, and just a little bit of reading can definitely save you weeks—if not months—of hardship.

Wednesday Recap: Heavy-Hitters Rotation

- Mycoinsecticides like BioCeres WP
- Pesticides like Pyrethrin
- EPA-Registered & Cannabis-Approved Chemistries

154

Thursdays: Scouting & Plant Work

Again, after applying chemistries on Wednesday, we need to go in there and make sure what we did is working and make sure that we don't have any spray damage.

Spend Thursday making sure that everything is the way it is supposed to be in terms of the applications methods, marking anything that is out of place, damaged, or otherwise needs attention.

Thursday Recap: Scouting & Plant Work

- Scouting
- Marking

Friday: The Final Blow

We recommend finishing your week off strong by rotating either an insecticidal soap, a sulfur-based product, or a citric acid product depending on the situation that you guys are dealing with.

Every situation is unique, so you wouldn't necessarily just want to use soap across the board.

If you are dealing with canopy-based insects like aphids, spider mites, white flies, to a certain degree, that insecticidal soap on Fridays is a very good option for you.

Sulfur would be great for a situation where your environment is just not working and you have PM that just keeps coming back; using a sulfur spray can help get you a little bit of prolonged efficacy in this situation.

Or let's say you are dealing with russet mites. Sulfur is very effective against russets as well, so that's where that would come in on a Friday rotation.

Citric acid is what I like to use for maintenance - it's a mold inhibitor, so it's going to keep things like mycelium from popping up in the canopy.

It's enough of an acid where it can help dissolve egg membranes before they hatch.

Plus, a lot of insects just don't like citric acid, so putting that out on Fridays, even if you don't see anything, is a good way to continue your preventative rather than curative approach.

Note: For Veg and Flower with OxiPhos

In terms of your SOP, make sure that you have OP on a 21-day rotation.

The ISR that is elicited is going to last for 3 weeks, starting prior to propagation:

1. Spray your moms
2. Spray your veg 1x or 2x depending on veg cycle length
3. Spray again at flip

CLEAN GROWING: INTEGRATED PEST MANAGEMENT FOR CANNABIS GROWERS

4. Then apply as a foliar spray in Week 3 and week 6 of Flower.

Assuming you are running a full 9-week cycle, you will have induced that systemic response from clone all the way to harvest and you will see much less instance of disease pressure in those healthy plants as a result.

Flower Phase

The flower schedule is very similar to the propagation and veg phases:

For the first 1-3 weeks of flower (up until day 21), continue to apply M/W/F rotation if you so desire.

Still adhere to taking clones on Tuesdays, doing your scouting on Thursdays, and Saturday and Sunday are hopefully minimal work and can enjoy some semblance of a weekend.

But once we get into about weeks 4-7, I really do recommend being very proactive because you're limited in your toolset.

In certain situations, you may want to employ biological controls later in flower so you don't have insect outbreaks. That is not advised if you have pathogen pressure.

Again, make sure that in that week 6 you are applying that OxiPhos and Zerotol together in a 1:300 to ensure ISR is elicited and potential contaminants sterilized.

Late Flower

In late flower when toolsets are limited, citric acid and ZeroTol are awesome spot treatments with minimal negative impact.

If you ever have any flare ups, those two are going to have the least effect on your potency and terpene profiles.

Citric acid is used in food so it is considered to be safe, and ZeroTol breaks down into oxygen and water, so there's not a whole lot of anything there that could ever make anyone sick.

Pre-Harvest

While controversial, as discussed earlier, one thing Zac always recommends commercially is a ZeroTol spray at 1:100 if your products are subjected to any type of microbial testing.

A 1:100 rate is a very indiscriminate rate as far as yeast, mold, and fungi which continue to plague cultivators post-harvest; ZeroTol is very effective against all 3 issues without having to risk a loss in potency.

Remember, if you are spraying, spray the plants before you cut them down rather than trying to do a post harvest dip to maintain osmotic pressure and avoid damage.

Cannabis is very much like a rose in terms of once that osmotic pressure has been severed, the petals or calyx can become damaged by moisture, whereas if they are still attached to the stem, you are going to see much less degradation.

Plus, you can't ever be accused of trying to cheat the system, because you are subjecting the entire crop to the same sanitary protocols.

It is not unethical to get in there the day of harvest and make sure that your trim team is cutting down something clean.

If your trimmers get there by 10:00, make sure application is done by 9:00 so that 1 hour REI lapses and you are compliant and cutting down a disinfested product.

Post-Harvest

For post-harvest facility disinfection, we recommend using a food safe option like Sanidate 5 with a biofoamer.

Sanidate at 1:100 will give you that food safety claim so that you meet the FDA requirements and have that ability to say that you are growing in a food safe environment.

With everything that's going on in the world today, it's not mandated yet, but it will be.

For irrigation lines, we like to use the Green Clean acid first,

let that sit for 1-2 hours, flush it out, and then apply Sani-Date at 1:100.

Let it sit overnight. Come back the next day and you will have gotten your system as close to "new" as the irrigation components can get.

If you still see peanut butter coming out of the lines, you may have to repeat this process multiple times depending on how old the system is and how big the bioburden may be.

We also recommend treating your water with ZT.

There are some good injectors out there—dosatron, anderson, argus—that will all allow you to use Zerotol to keep your lines clean in the process and not have to worry about emitters not working midway through because of the stuff that has accumulated during the cycle.

A few notes about this SOP:

- Don't use RO for your sprays because reverse osmosis water does not have any bicarbonate or buffer capability to it.

- So, if you are using something like ZT, you are going to notice the pH drop out, and you're going to want to bring it back up. But if you mix something like potassium hydroxide and PAA together, they cancel each other out, and you've basically

160

made very expensive water at that point.

- We recommend using a water source with ~0.3EC for sprays.

- If you don't have the ability to use tap water, or you have very dirty well water and you use RO, you can add something like 1/10th strength NPK fertilizer in there to try to get you to about 0.3 EC to give you enough of a buffer to where it is not going to bottom out the spray pH right away.

- Zac always recommends spraying early in the day.

  Let your lights come on for like an hour. Turn off the row you are spraying. So on and so forth throughout the room.

  That way you are attacking insects while they are mobile and you are addressing any pathogens while you get a dry down period during the day.

- For mold and mildew, spraying early is advantageous because the desiccation from the daytime is going to bring that relative humidity down and make an inhospitable environment for mold and mildew.

- For insects, they are going to be most awake after lights come on and they are going to be mobile. So, the chance of them coming in contact with whatever you are putting out goes way up.

- It is not recommended to mix something like ZeroTol with something like BioCeres; or Sanidate with ZeroTol. Combining microbials and disinfesting creates very expensive water.

CHAPTER ELEVEN

Mother Plant Care & Maintenance SOP

Successful Cycles Start With Healthy Moms

For the healthiest start, you need healthy moms.

Healthy moms give you healthy cuttings.
Healthy cuttings give you healthy clones.
Healthy clones give you healthy veg plants.
Healthy veg plants give you healthy flower plants.

"If momma ain't happy, ain't nobody happy."

This topic was actually requested online during the Fireside series that Zac hosted for BioSafe Systems' instagram.

What follows are some specific recommendations, and some basic Do's & Don'ts, so you can confidently take it from there.

First and foremost, take care of your moms.

Love your moms like they are your mom because they are responsible for your success.

Mother plants are really the basis of any successful grow, so don't neglect them.

Make sure that she is getting the care that she needs because if you don't have good moms, you won't have good clones. And if you don't have good clones, you're going to be fighting an uphill battle for the rest of the process.

We typically recommend selecting a mother plant from seed if given the option because this gives you something called "hybrid vigor."

Hybrid vigor from a seed mom is unmatched for a clone. When you pop a seed, you are going to have the most vigor you could possibly have, and that's going to translate to healthier, more vigorous clones as well.

Over time, that vigor wanes, and the further you get from that initial seed, the more certain varieties can be impacted.

Something that Zac likes to do with his seed moms before he ever flowers them out is to take clones off of them, get those clones to a teen phase. Grow those cuts out, and by the time you can tell whether to keep the mother plant or not, you have another round ready to go.

While our understanding is still very much in its early stages, we do know that epigenetics plays a role in cannabis, and that the further you get away from that initial seed, the more it is like making a copy of a copy of a copy of a copy.

That being said, it is possible to keep very vigorous healthy mothers from both clones and seeds, there's just a few key things that you need to pay attention to:

First: With mother plants, drain to waste.

Not just a little runoff to the bottom. You want to take the watering capacity of your container, and you want to feed that plus maybe 5-10% to be able to leach out the exudates that the plant has put out.

A lot of times mother plants are in the largest container that they are going to get. Very few people up-pot their mother plants after the fact. Some do, and that's cool, but the majority of folks basically put a mother plant in a pot and that's where it will stay until it is no longer a mother plant.

Second: How long should you keep moms? Typically 90 days.

After ~3 months, we recommend you rejuvenate your stable (flower your mom out and replace with another).

Moms make great flowering plants because they have been wanting to do it for a while, plus, it helps to keep those fresh green cuttings coming because we all know, the longer a mother plant stays around, the woodier the cuttings get and woody cuttings take longer to root.

By cycling out your moms effectively, you are going to make sure that you are not seeing any of those prolonged rooting times that could set your operation behind.

There really is no wrong way to raise them. I've seen 8 ft tall plants and char-cored blocks. I've seen bushes in 100-gallon pots. It's all about however long that grower chooses to keep it.

But I feel like that 3-month time window give or take is good for cycling it out. This way, every quarter you are putting new mother stock into your nursery and you're able to push those genetics to their full potential.

Third: Use the right media for your moms; something that buffers and allows drainage.

Zac's personal preference is to keep mother plants in a potting soil/coco mix, rather than purely one or the other:

- Potting soil provides an organic charge to the mix, reducing the chances of you running into micronutrient issues, and it has a very high cation exchange capability as well, so when you inoculate that plant with nutrients, you know that you will have a little bit of reserve from that potting soil.

- The advantage to mixing with coco is that coco is quick draining, won't necessarily go acidic on you, and it provides a good organic structure for microbes, great in cases where you aren't transplanting (like mother plants in their final pots).

What about mothering clones in rockwool?

Your media should be in proportion to your irrigation; I've seen 8ft tall plants out of a 2-gallon pot that were just irrigated frequently, and the grower made sure the root mass had ample osmotic pressure to provide what was going up to the canopy and there was no larf or unnecessary growth going up those plants.

So, it is possible to put it in rockwool, but because of the tendency for growers to put mother plants in corners and neglect them, rockwool has the highest chance of having issues if you are not diligent.

Fourth: Make sure you have good enzymatic activity in your root zone to avoid exudate buildups that lock out nutrient uptake.

Something like TerraGrow is going to introduce microbes that exude enzymes, giving you the benefit of the microbes adhering to your roots, and also the enzymatic activity in the form of the exudates that are crucial to keeping your mom's roots healthy and happy.

With a mother plant, this is essential because roots are going to grow, and die, new roots are going to grow and you don't want dead organic material in a pot that you are not going to up pot.

For any of our growers that are in a peat-based media, even straight up potting soil that has peat moss in it, you may want to look into products like CalOx, which help growers raise the pH of their media in the case of exudate (salt) buildup.

So, if you've got a mother plant that's hanging around in a container for a prolonged period of time, it's building up that exudate and you need to basically be able to bring the pH up of that media immediately. Something like CalOx is a liquid limestone product that can bring your pH up immediately by 1 point for a period of about 30 days.

When used in conjunction with dolomitic lime, you're going to be able to have that immediate elicitation so that your plant can uptake nutrients, and then, as that dolomitic lime begins to break down and become available, that mother plant is going to be able to sustain herself for a longer period of time because of that longer term pH correction.

Last: With mother plants, I always recommend spraying them rather than spraying your clones.

Your mother plants are going to be heartier and more established, making them better apt to deal with stress. Sprays and applications won't stress a hearty mature plant out, but that could be a kiss of death to a fresh clone.

So, when you're talking about creating a giant wound on a young cutting, the last thing you would want to do is subject it to more undue stress.

That Monday/Wednesday/Friday spray schedule then comes in clutch because Tuesdays you can take clones, and Thursdays, you're doing plant maintenance. That allows you to get on a consistent rotation where you are always making sure you know what's going on in the garden.

Spray those moms before you take those cuts: OxiPhos and ZeroTol are a great spray for the mother plant before you take your clones.

This combo is going to disinfect the cuttings as well as impart that ISR for that 21-day period into the cutting, so that after 14 days they have rooted out and you still have a week for them to acclimate to their new environment with that stress response elicited before you need to spray again.

Pay attention to what your mother plants are telling you.

Plants talk and sometimes mother plants are going to almost flower because of the fact that they get so bushy and there's not enough light getting into that canopy.

If you've had a mother plant that's gotten to that point, you're going to have more issues than benefits from it. If you are getting to a point where you are seeing a lot of preflowers—not just the normal two calyxes shooting out as it grows but clusters—it's time; she wants to grow.

And if you flip her at that point you are going to have a decent harvest out of her.

I know that mother plants aren't necessarily the easiest to manage, but at the same time don't forget them, they've got you to where you are.

Also, if you live in a state where you are able to obtain seeds legally, we advise that you do so, both for genetic preservation and to regularly have a pool of genetics to dip into and recapture that hybrid vigor.

There are a lot of varieties out there that are "clone-only," but seeds allow you to set yourself apart from the game.

Every new flavor that comes out, that's somebody popping a seed in a basement or a facility somewhere. We can think about what was going on yesterday and get on that hype train, or we can find our own.

So, in Zac's personal opinion, buy seeds over clones, because you are going to be able to have access to stuff that isn't necessarily available to the market to begin with. And then, you can mom out your own seeds and get multiple, successful cycles.

Mother plants are quintessential to being able to have a successful harvest from start to finish. Take care of your mom. She will take care of you, if you take care of her.

I often get asked:

When selecting a clone for a mother, is there anything to look for in particular to help offset loss of hybrid vigor from seed?

If you take 6 cuts, and 5 of them are to be put into production, hold the one that's the most vigorous back for the mother plant.

After about 3 months, that's when she gets flipped into the mix and you take that next most vigorous cutting and that's your new mom. By selecting the best branch, so to speak, you're going to ensure that the gradual vigor drift is minimized as best you can.

Mother Plant Quick SOP

3-Part Process: ZeroTol, OxiPhos, TerraGrow

1. Use OP on mother plants before you take your clones to impart 21-day residual ISR.
2. Apply OP+ZT every 3 weeks for moms and veg plants.
3. Apply TG every 2 weeks for moms and veg plants.

Treat mother plants, elicit that ISR throughout the rooting phase of your clone's life, and then hit them with another OP application once rooted to get them through veg.

Then, hit them at flip, and again in Week 3 and Week 6 of flower.

Assuming you're running a 9-week cycle, that gives you ISR from propagation to harvest with the utilization of OP's potassium phosphate molecule. This molecule is what elicits the ISR without leaving any harmful residuals that can be imparted into the plant or final product.

CHAPTER TWELVE

Propagation & Cloning SOPs

The Grow Guy's Cloning SOP

Propagation and cloning is one of the most integral parts of any grow because it is what sets up your next subsequent rounds for success, or failure.

You need to make sure you're taking good care of your moms, because starting on a solid foundation is going to allow you to have better propagation results and healthier veg plants, which means better flowering plants.

Make sure that you are treating your mother plants before you ever take clones.

173

Clones are already under one of the most stressful situations you can put a plant through – they have literally been severed from their root system and have to start from scratch.

The more you spray your cuts, the more detriment you're going to cause to those clones, which is why any IPM applications should be done in advance of taking cuttings.

Anything you can do ahead of time to mitigate issues on the mom before you take your cuts is going to translate to healthier clones in the long run.

To do this, we use Zac's personal favorite mix (ZeroTol+OP+AG) the day before cloning:

- **ZeroTol makes sure conditions are sterile.** If there were any negative microbes or biology present, It's addressed ahead of time so we are not just spreading stuff to our clone domes.
- **OxiPhos elicits that 21-day ISR** protection against pathogens and disease, which carries over to our clones.
- **AzaGuard gives the plants a repellency** quality.

In practice:

1. Monday: ZeroTol + OxiPhos + Azaguard together on your mother plants
2. Tuesday: We take our cuts of inoculated clones that have an ISR protection for 21 days

By following this practice, you are removing that conducive environment for problems, and your clones are going to have the best chance against whatever pests or pathogens may find their way in.

A clean cloning SOP also makes a huge difference for anyone that is selling clones.

You can say, "Hey, I make sure that these clones have a 21-day disease resistance imparted into them" before you give that to a customer, and that customer is going to have a piece of mind knowing that ISR is going to be giving them that residual protection.

Cloning Media

In terms of media for clones, it's all over the board as far as how people like to do it:

- Grodan and rockwool cubes
- Aeroponic cloning machines
- Rapid rooters and jiffy pellets (peat style rooting media)
- Germination mixes that people use

And, really, it's all anecdotal as far as which media is "best"; the best media is the one that works the best for you.

Whichever media you seem to have the most success with, I say go with that one because there's a thousand different recipes for chili, and just because somebody is having success cloning in a certain fashion does not necessarily mean that it is going to be conducive to the way you do things.

Zac's Preference: 4" Rockwool cubes with 4 Cuttings per cube.

Take a Delta-4 Cube (the 4" rockwool Grodan), and poke a hole in each of the corners with a pencil.

Then, you can do 4 cuttings per block, limiting the amount of media that you have to have in a tray at any given amount of time, making it easy to rehydrate.

Once everything is rooted out, they are easy to split up — just take a razor blade once everything is rooted out, slice your cube into 4 sections, and you've got 4 decent-sized clones.

The reason I use the Delta-4 is you've got 4 inches of rooting media, so you can take a 7" clone and stick it 3" into that block and still have a little bit of space for the roots to proliferate out and possibly skip a week or two in your veg cycle because you've taken a giant clone.

A lot of people like to use aeroponic cloning methods, and if they work for you, stick with what works.

An old trick that we used to do in California when we were using them, especially in the summer months when it gets hot, was to take old glass bottles, freeze them and throw them in the reservoir to offset the heat of the pump without having to worry about changing the pH or EC of the cloner.

To keep your cloner sterile, we recommend doing Sanidate treatments at a 1:100 application rate in between runs to thoroughly disinfect your pumps, collars, and spray heads.

Sterilizing and disinfesting between runs is probably the best way to make sure you are going to continue to have success with your propagation in that fashion. Because aeroponic cloners don't really have "media" per se, they're ripe for pathogens and pests that love dissolved oxygen with no resistance.

Anywhere roots grow quickly, other things can grow quickly in that environment as well, such as pathogens and pests.

If you have your aeroponic setup dialed in and that's the way you like to do it, just make sure that you're staying sterile, in and out of the reservoir.

Note: *Some growers like to apply a ZeroTol misting application on the tops of their clones to help alleviate problems caused by excess moisture. This can help, but I wouldn't recommend doing that more than once per clone cycle, and would be at a maintenance rate of 1:256.*

A lot of folks like to clone with rapid rooters or peat pellets, and it's a very successful way to clone.

Peat pellets can go into pretty much any system, and they are biodegradable. Peat itself is held together with a polymer and its an optimal air to water ratio for cloning.

The only downside I've seen to peat pellets is that they don't really provide a lot of support as far as upper growth vs. root mass; you could have a 10" tall clone growing out of a 2.5" peat pellet. At that point, proportions are off.

If you are going to use peat pellets or rapid rooters, I advise taking smaller cuttings to avoid that tip over that can be inevitable in those situations.

Repurpose. Reuse. Recycle.

Some folks don't necessarily like rockwool because they think it is not biodegradable, but, again, it is just spun rock.

It is not synthetic or artificial, and it's not going to hurt the earth. It was stuff that was here; we just changed its form.

If you live in a dry climate like Colorado like I do, something you can do to be more sustainable in your efforts is take your old rockwool blocks, bust them up, and till them in your garden, and that will actually help you with aspects like water retention.

First, you used your media to help get your clones to fruition, now it's keeping the garden wet.

Air-Pruning Propagation

Another method to take clones that Zac learned in Jamaica that blew our minds was basically an adapted air-pruning style of cloning.

Zac met a gentleman at Orange Hill who said he'd never lost a clone in his life. He takes plastic bags, ties them on the V (the point where main stalk meets the branch), and basically root his clones on the mother plant.

By rooting them on the mother plant, he has a second viable plant before he ever severs osmotic pressure.

He can plant it, and it's good to go; I thought that was genius.

Cutting Angles

Most growers cause too much stress when taking their cuts.

The old rule of thumb has always been 45° angle cuts on your clones because (in theory) it exposes the most surface area for new roots. Others suggest splitting the stem in half with a blade to further expose for roots.

There are a hundred different ways farmers will take cuts off their mother plants, but I will tell you guys:

- Don't do 45's

- Don't split your stem
- Don't mangle your cuttings

The more damage you inflict on that young plant, the longer it is going to take it to heal before it ever focuses on any type of growth.

If 45° is the most surface area we can possibly expose on that cutting, doing that angled cut creates the biggest wound possible for that plant to heal.

If you are able to do a straight cut across the bottom, you are going to see roots 2-3 days faster because that's an easier wound for the plant to heal.

Plants are always going to heal before they focus on growth.

Please don't split your stems. Please don't scrape down to the xylem and phloem. Please don't do 45° cuts. Do a straight across cut, and let her heal faster so she can root faster.

Cloning Nutrition & Gels

Typically, if your mothers are healthy, the clone will have enough nutrition to get itself to a phase where it can root.

Until those roots are developed, doing a light foliar feed would really be your only option, but again the more you spray those plants, the worse they are going to look.

So, instead, just cut those clones off of healthy moms and you won't really need to worry about having to do any mild fertilization during that quick period where they are rooting out.

As soon as they are planted up, start doing it, but during the time when they are just in the block/cloner/plugs/etc., just let them do their thing.

A lot of growers like cloning gel, and have found it to be very effective. I've seen others have great success using only aloe.

In our last few runs, we have used local honey and it has worked just as good as cloning gels.

The idea is to create something that can seal that wound you've created on the bottom, and honey is antiseptic that helps prevent embolism from occurring.

Honey and aloe are a great way to propagate plants without having to utilize any synthetic hormones (popular gels often use indole-3-butyric acid, for example), which is typically only used for propagating ornamentals, not edible crops.

The moral of the story is no matter which way you choose to propagate your cuttings, use what works for you, and make sure that you are treating your mother plants ahead of time to ensure that your clones will have the most successful route possible.

The more you mess with them, the worse they will look.

Get into a routine where you can set it and forget it, and hopefully within 10-14 days you are into your next cycle, up-potting, taking new clones, and off to the races.

CHAPTER THIRTEEN

IPM & Plant Care Workflow Calendar

What It All Looks Like Together

Over the next few pages you will find complete, day-by-day and week-by-week summaries of the SOPs discussed for quick reference in your grow or facility.

Including:

- Veg Stage
- Flower Stage
- Cloning & Propagation
- Mother Plant Care
- Example Full Workflow Calendar

VEG + FLOWER SOPs

VEG STAGE						
Day	Monday	Tuesday	Wednesday	Thursday	Friday	Sat/Sun
Action:	Weaken	Clone	Heavy Hitters	Scouting	Finisher	Minimal
Products/Tasks	AG+ZT OP (every 3 weeks)	Cloning Scouting Defoliation Sticky Cards Flags	BioCeres Myco Insecticides Pyrethrin Spinosad (Rotate 3-4 tools)	Look for efficacy of treatment Sticky card counts Look for damage from treatments	Insecticidal Soap Sulfur-Based Product Citric-Acid Based Product Ex: Nuke Em or SOS209	
METHOD:	SPRENCH	Mechanical	SPRENCH	Mechanical	SPRAY	N/A

FLOWER STAGE	
Week 1 - Week 3	Same as Veg Cycle
Week 4 - Week 6	Be Proactive
Week 6 - Week 7	OxiPhos + Zerotol (1:300 application rate; Sprench)
Week 7 - Late Flower	Citric Acid or Zerotol for Spot Treatment (1:100 application rate; sprayed)
PRE HARVEST (1 Hour Before)	Spray entire crop with ZeroTol (1:100 application rate, sprayed)

CLEAN GROWING: INTEGRATED PEST MANAGEMENT FOR CANNABIS GROWERS

CLONING + PROPAGATION + MOMS

CLONING & PROPAGATION	
Day 0 (day before cuts taken)	Treat moms with Zerotol & OxiPhos (1:300 of each; Sprench)
Day 1	Take Clones; Cutting dip 1:250; recommend mass dunk rather than one at a time
Once Rooted	TerraGrow (1:250 rate; drench)
Transplant Dunks	TerraGrow Slurry (3 grams/10 gal; slurry dunks of plugs or cubes)
Bi-Weekly Follow-Ups	Terragrow (0.5-1.0 grams/gallon; drench)

MOM CARE (Cycle Moms every 3-6 Months when possible)	
Every 3 Weeks	Treat moms with Zerotol & OxiPhos (1:300 of each; Sprench)
Every 2 Weeks	Terragrow (0.5-1.0 grams/gallon; drench)

185

EXAMPLE CALENDAR: WORKFLOW + IPM

	TASK	Monday	Tuesday	Wednesday	Thursday	Friday	Saturday/Sunday
Week 1 VEG	IPM	Azaguard/oxyphos/zerotol	Nothing advised Team evaluate pre spray, cleaning	Heavy hitter (pyganic, mycoinsecticides)	Nothing advised	Suppression/support (Citric acid, soap, sulfur)	Nothing advised.
	Work Flow	Set up weekly tasks/cleaning/spraying		Spraying/cleaning	Cleaning/Scouting	Cleaning/weekly wrap up/spraying	
Week 2 VEG	IPM	Azaguard/zerotol tank mix	Nothing Advised	Heavy hitter (pyganic, mycoinsecticides)	Foliar feed if needed	Suppression/support (Citric acid, soap, sulfur)	Nothing Advised
	Work Flow	Set up weekly tasks/cleaning/spraying	Team evaluation of garden/cleaning/defoliation	Spraying/cleaning	Cleaning/Scouting	Cleaning/weekly wrap up/spraying	
Week 3 Veg/Moms	IPM	Azaguard/zerotol tank mix	Nothing Advised Cut clones/evaluation/cleaning	Heavy hitter (pyganic, mycoinsecticides)	Nothing advised	Suppression/support (Citric acid, soap, sulfur) Spraying/Transplant/Weekly wrap up	Nothing Advised
	Work Flow	Set up weekly tasks/cleaning/spraying		Spraying/cleaning	Cleaning/Scouting		
Weeks 1-3 Flower	IPM	Azaguard/oxyphos/zerotol	Nothing Advised	Heavy hitter (pyganic, mycoinsecticides)	Nothing advised	Suppression/support (Citric acid, soap, sulfur)	Nothing advised
	Work Flow	Set up weekly tasks/cleaning/spraying. Defoliate plants at flip and again at day 21.	Team evaluation of garden/cleaning/Defoliation	Spraying/cleaning	Cleaning/Scouting	Cleaning/weekly wrap up/spraying	
Weeks 4-6	IPM	Zerotol and Citric acid as needed. Reapply oxyphos/zt combo in week 4. *This is the time to use beneficial insects	Nothing Advised	As needed	Nothing advised	As needed	Nothing Advised
	Work Flow	Set up weekly tasks/cleaning/spraying	Team evaluation of garden/cleaning/Defoliation	Spraying/cleaning	Cleaning/Scouting	Cleaning/weekly wrap up/spraying	
Weeks 7-9	IPM	Zerotol and Citric acid as needed. Preharvest zerotol spray recommended.	Nothing advised Team of evaluation of garden/cleaning / pre harvest defoliation	As needed	Nothing advised	As needed	Nothing advised
	Work Flow	Set up weekly tasks/cleaning/spraying/pre harvest defoliation		Spraying/cleaning/harvest	Cleaning/Scouting/harvest	Cleaning/weekly wrap up/spraying/harvest	

CHAPTER FOURTEEN

Bringing in New Genetics SOP

Introducing New Genetics Without Contaminating Your Grow

New flavors and varieties allow growers to avoid existing systemic problems, passed down from cycle to cycle indefinitely.

However, introducing new plants into your grow can increase your risks of contaminants, pests and pathogens—from one grow to another, or even room to room.

Proper quarantine procedures allow growers to isolate and identify issues beforehand, so that they are not transplanting problems from one space to another.

For the longest time, growers were limited to what was in the system, and you were essentially buying someone else's problem.

Clones would have spider mites, thrips, etc.; It was just part of the game.

The easiest way to introduce new genetics with less risk is popping new seeds.

But that isn't always an option.

It'd be nice to start from seed every time, but you could have a power outage in veg and lose your whole grow, and if you have to start from seed, that means you go bankrupt waiting for your final product.

We recommend a dedicated quarantine space, as far from your main grow as possible.

Try to have an area in your environment that is as far off the beaten path as possible. Ideally, you want to be using an auxiliary door to get to said room so don't have to even walk through the facility with your new plants.

The more rooms you walk by—every single door you walk by—is a chance for contamination.

Even the periphery of the building, property, or grow can be a source of contamination.

188

How to Quarantine Plants & Introduce New Genetics (SOP)

1. Set up a tent or greenhouse depending on your environment and how many plants you are bringing in.
2. Put the plants in this space and start a 3-week quarantine.
3. Integrate normal IPM, including root and foliar treatments.
4. After 3 weeks, take clones off of the plants that you brought into your quarantine environment. Ideally, you'll want to put these clones in a separate environment from both your quarantine and your main grow area.
5. Root your clones, get them into veg, and, if you aren't noticing any issues, the plants are most likely clean. If you notice problems with your clones, you may need to backtrack, going back to the quarantined mother plants, cleaning them again, and getting new, clean clones.

Never introduce plants given to you by others directly into your grow.

Take a clone of that plant and toss the original. If a plant has problems like root aphid pressure, for example, it's hard to get out of the media itself, whereas a root aphid isn't going to be on the top of a clean clone."

It's important to keep your quarantined plants and clones away from other sources of pests, pathogens, and threats.

This ensures the anything observed is systemic to the genetics or source and not a product of the environment that they are introduced into.

What about sulfur dips?

While some swear by a sulfur dip, these can be ineffective and inconsistent methods for plant treatment.

Sulfur dips are only as effective as the guy doing it.

A poor gentleman who has 900 plants is not going to be giving all of them the same attention.

The larger the grow, the less attention the last plants get.

CHAPTER FOURTEEN

IPM FAQs

The Most Frequently Asked Questions from Zac's Fireside Chats

Q. Can Zerotol 2.0 and Zerotol HC be used at the same rate?

A. Yes we recommend the same applications for both (1:100 for curative; 1:256 for maintenance.)

Q. How many mL/gal for a ZeroTol root drench?

A. For ZeroTol, use a sprench method to spray the tops of containers unless you have a root-borne disease. For your media, 1:100-1:256 for curative treatments.

191

If the idea is to keep more pathogens at bay, you can also treat with AzaGuard (4 mL/gal as a sprench) and BioCeres WP (7-9 grams/gal for a sprench) where you hit the canopy as well as the root ball.

For water treatment, use 1.2 mL/Gal of ZeroTol to remove food before it gets to the media. This is being proactive vs. reactive and I advocate water treatment whenever possible.

Q. What is the average cost to start using BioSafe?

A. BioSafe products are priced for farmers, and they do not put the cannabis tax on their chemistries. Whether you are a hobby grower, poinsettia grower, or potato grower, you pay the same price. Everyone is on team BioSafe, and no one has an unfair advantage. Our professional products are available in retail sizes, such as 2.5 gallons of ZeroTol 2.0 compared to 1 gallon of hydrogen peroxide. We also offer 2.5 gallons of OMRI herbicide, as well as retail versions.

Q. What is the ZeroTol Foliar Pre-Harvest rate?

A. If you see active heavy disease pressure or are addressing microbial contamination before harvest, the ZeroTol Foliar Preharvest rate is 37 mL/gal. For maintenance purposes, the rate is 15 mL/gal.

Q. Can you mix ZeroTol with RO water?

A. It is not recommended to mix ZeroTol with RO water, as the lack of bicarbonate in RO water can cause the pH to bottom out. ZeroTol can drop the pH of RO water to 3.0, and when pH up is added without bicarbonate, it can render ZeroTol less effective. If tap water quality is poor, use a mixture of tap water and RO water at a ratio of 1:10. The pH should be between 5-7 and allowed to stabilize.

Q. Can you mix ZeroTol and BioCeres?

A. It is not recommended to mix ZeroTol and BioCeres, as ZeroTol is a disinfest product while BioCeres is a fungal spore and fungicide. Mixing the two products can render them both ineffective. Instead, it is suggested to use AzaGuard and ZeroTol on Monday, and BioCeres on Wednesday, to address multiple issues and "kick them while they are down."

Q. What is the recommended advice on clone dipping?

A. The recommended clone dipping advice is to use 15ml of ZeroTol without RO water. It is important to note that cannabis plants are similar to roses in terms of osmotic pressure, so petal wetness and petal burn may occur, similar to the effects of H2O2 and PAA on cannabis plants. It is recommended to avoid dunking the plant after harvest as this is where degradation is most noticeable. Instead, a sprinkler can be used next to the plant to avoid petal burn. It is advised to treat plants while they are still growing to avoid any accusations of cheating a sample.

Q. What is the average shelf life of IPM products when stored properly?

A. The average shelf life of IPM (Integrated Pest Management) products is 12-18 months when stored properly.

Q. How do I determine how much of each IPM product to buy?

A. A good metric is to use 1 gallon of solution for 400 sq ft with a 12" canopy depth. Multiply that by how many sprays you plan to do to determine how much of a particular product you need. This calculation will give you an idea of how many quarts of a product will last for a specific amount of time.

Q. What should I do if I miss a day of IPM applications? Should I try to catch up by doing all of those applications with today's treatments?

A. If you miss a day of IPM applications, it's important to remember that yesterday is gone and you can't change it. If you try to do yesterday's treatments today, the snowball effect can cause delays to get worse. We are all human, so if you miss a day, just do better tomorrow.

Q: What is the recommended mixture for treating russet on plants?

A: The best mixture for russet treatment includes AzaGuard as an antifeedant, anti-grow, and anti-egg solution, mycoinsecticides such as BioCeres and PFR97, and micronized sulfur.

Q: How do I use Green Clean Acid Cleaner/sulfuric acid?

A: Basically, it's used as step 1 in cleaning a DWC system. The acid cleaner works like sandpaper to rough up and break loose any deposits in the system. To use it, dilute at a 1:100 ratio and run for 1-2 hours. Then, flush the system with 2x the amount of clear water it holds. Next, fill the system with Sanidate 5.0 at a 1:100 ratio and let it sit for 3 hours (overnight is best). The next day, flush the system with 2x the amount of clear water again. Finally, put the net pots back in and you should have a system as close to clean as possible. This process can be used for cleaning both DWC and drip line systems.

Q: Can you fog ZeroTol late in flower?

A: Yes, many growers will do a pre-harvest ZeroTol treatment for any microbial concerns at a 1:100 rate. ZeroTol is effective against yeast, mold, and fungi. ZeroTol is a zero-residual chemistry, meaning it won't leave anything behind that could affect the taste, flavor, or potency of the plant. It only contains oxygen and water. This treatment can help cut down on the need for other cleaning products. The re-entry interval (REI) for ZeroTol is 1 hour. It's best to apply it right before harvest. Remember, any other farmer who wants to sell their produce in a grocery store would have to do this treatment for human pathogen testing.

Q: What about preventive measures for scale insects?

A: Dealing with scale infestations can be pretty unpleasant. I've had to deal with European elm scale when I lived in Northern California and grew in the redwoods, and it was just a result of the environment. What I have found to be the most effective against scale is an oil-based product, such as mineral oil or something that contains garlic oil—a 25B or EPA registered oil. Essentially, we have to suffocate them, which is one of the only ways to kill them. There are some systemic products that can also eliminate them, but they are not safe for use on cannabis. Therefore, oil-based products are the best approach for this crop type.

Q: What beneficials should we use in our garden?

A: For soil microbes, use bacillus, trichoderma, azobacter, and to a lesser degree, some mycorrhizal. In your actual canopy, clonostachys rosea is an awesome microbe. For insect mitigation, consider using everything from Phytoseiulus persimilis to californicus to lacewing to assassin bug.

Doing your scouting is crucial so that you can put out the right amount and type of bugs. For example, if you had thrips but put out persimilis, that's not going to do anything for you. It is a waste of money because the persimilis mites will starve to death and die because they don't have a food source. The end goal is for your beneficials to starve out because there isn't a food source, but throwing a beneficial into an environment where there isn't even prey present is a waste of money. Ensure that your scouting is beneficial to your releases so that you are getting a tailored approach towards the situation that you are dealing with.

Q: What surfactants or foliars do you prefer?

A: For situations like botrytis, I prefer a nonionic surfactant like CocoWet or Natural Wet. When dealing with mite outbreaks, canopy aphids, and PM, I am a big fan of organosilicone spreader stickers like Capsil. It really depends on the situation and whether coverage or permeation is going to be the issue. If coverage is the issue, I would recommend using an organisilicone, whereas if permeation is the issue, a nonionic surfactant would be more suitable.

Q: Which cultivars do you like to grow?

A: Zac is a fan of anything that has chocolate terps. He also enjoys growing some of the older strains, but is not as fond of the new varieties. They are often difficult to distinguish from one another due to similar lineage and flower structure.

His top three favorite strains of all time are: The Wookies, bred by Phil Hague, Black Widow from Mr. Nice, and the old school Sour D that he got from his friend Mike in Santa Cruz years ago.

(Shoutout to the Gardening Unlimited crew, Vondo, and all those guys).

Q: Can I mix BioCeres and AzaGuard with ZeroTol and foaming agent and apply?

A: Yes, you can mix BioCeres and AzaGuard, or AzaGuard and ZeroTol, but do not ever mix BioCeres and ZeroTol. BioCeres is an entomopathogenic fungus, and ZeroTol is a fungicide. So, you're basically canceling out both products. Even though you can tank mix AzaGuard and BioCeres, I typically don't recommend it. Use your AzaGuard and follow up in 2-3 days with the BioCeres so that you're playing off the antifeedant quality, the growth regulation, and the ovicidal properties of the AzaGuard. Basically, we are weakening the insect before we hit them with the heavy hitter. By doing that, we are weakening the population as a whole and minimizing the potential for certain individuals in said population to become resistant to the method we are using to try to eliminate them.

Q: Do I recommend the foamer with cannabis plants?

A: It depends on your situation. I would not recommend it as the only application method, but it can be effective in certain situations where coverage might be an issue.

Generally, I would recommend using the foamer during the vegetative or early flowering stages. However, you should avoid foaming established flowers, as soap can cause premature degradation of the flower.

For example, if you have had a persistent spider mite infestation for the last three weeks, and spraying has not been effective, you can use the biofoaming agent with AzaGuard, OxiPhos, ZeroTol, pyrethrin, citric acid, sulfur, and insecticidal soap. It's best to stay away from oils or biologicals with the foamer because the soap can negatively affect the biologicals and cause phyto to occur.

Utilizing the foamer once a week in veg or early flower can be an option to ensure complete coverage and treatment of everything. Use 4oz per gallon of the biofoaming agent and follow the lower end of the label rate of the chemistry that you are mixing with the biofoaming agent, as well as adhere to the PPE on the said chemistry.

For example, if we are foaming ZeroTol, we want to make sure we have gloves, long sleeves, long pants, eye protection, shoes, and socks. Keep in mind that you are defaulting to whatever chemistries you are mixing's PPE because the biofoaming agent itself does not have an REI or PPE requirements.

Q: What about dish soap and oil-based products, can you do a drench?

A: Definitely not. You should never put any oil on your root zone. It will cause a hydrophobic layer that will adhere to the outer portion of your root, and any time water comes through, you might be able to absorb some of it, but you're definitely going to see ill effects from drenching oils. Please, please do not do that.

Q: Can you use BioCeres for a drench?

A: Yes, you can. Typically, the sweet spot for BioCeres is going to be between 9-12 grams per gallon. With drenches, I typically recommend trying to do an irrigation first so that whatever insects you are going after become complacent, they get used to the moisture, and they are not going to be as apt to run away from the drench at that point. So we are able to target them a little bit more effectively and since they are used to the fact that the environment is already moist, they're not going to see that incoming pesticide drench as a threat necessarily.

Q: What kind of respirator should you use with PAA?

A: There is no respirator requirement for ZeroTol and Sanidate. However, if you want to take extra precautions and wear additional personal protective equipment, that is always a good idea. Generally, a half mask respirator that is rated for organic vapors is suitable for any biosafe product. As long as your P95 has an organic vapor rating on the cartridge, that is what you should look for. While it is not necessary for PAA, an ounce of prevention is a pound of cure. If wearing a respirator makes you feel safer, then you should do it since you are the applicator.

Q: What about bud rot, any treatment?

A: There is definitely a treatment for bud rot. We like to mix a nonionic surfactant such as Coco Wet, or something with a yucca saponin base with ZeroTol at a 1% solution (1:100, 37 ml/gal).

The reason we use a nonionic surfactant is that it is very effective at penetrating and permeating the cola. Since botrytis grows from the inside out, we need to ensure that we disinfest all the way to the stem. By using ZeroTol with a nonionic surfactant, we get the soaking action we need and ensure contact with those spores. While ZeroTol won't disinfect anything it doesn't touch, if it comes in contact with it, it will oxidize it and render it no longer viable. Using the 1% nonionic as close to harvest as possible, as well as manually opening the colas with a popsicle stick to introduce more oxygen into your environment is a good practice. Botrytis is an anaerobic microbe, so if we introduce oxygen into the environment, we can take away that conducive environment portion of the Triangle. If the environment is not right for the botrytis to grow, even if the spores may be present, they are not able to germinate, propagate, and decimate. Therefore, my recommendation would be to use that product as close to harvest as possible for that type of situation.

Q: Do a lot of bigger rec grows ever have preventative maintenance or IPM issues?

A: It depends on the rec grow. If you have a giant facility, you have to realize that spraying and scouting are just as important as watering your plants because you've created a perfect environment with no natural predators. You have to be the alpha predator in that situation and make sure that anything that does make its way in, you're the one eliminating it because mother nature has no influence in a warehouse. There are some big grows that do encounter issues. Every farmer is going to have some type of something pop up at some point. Being able to have a plan and move forward and institute protocols that will allow them to mitigate those issues is crucial. Every grow has issues, regardless of the size; it's just how you deal with those issues that determines whether or not you're going to have a successful harvest and be around next round.

Q: Do you (Zac) implement KNF into your garden?

A: I do not. I'm a synganics guy. I'm a fan of using mineral nutrition in conjunction with organics, amino acids, fulvic acids, and oligosaccharides.

Q: If you spray and do IPM every week, what are the chances you get pests and diseases?

A: I can't quantify it with a number, but the likelihood of you running into an issue is dramatically reduced because you're being proactive rather than reactive.

Q: What are some recommended teas for pest control?

A: My favorite is anything high in chitin, such as crab and shrimp shell meal. The theory is that it works like silica or calcium to strengthen cell walls, making it harder for insects to feed. Using homemade compost tea or other microbial teas can also be effective, but it can be difficult to replicate results unless you have an analysis of what the worms in the compost are eating and putting out, as not all microbes are created equal.

202

Q: How can we control algae and fungus gnats in the same application?

A: For mitigating pythium, use Zerotol as a drench. There's a good chance of root rot if there are fungus gnats present, so use ZeroTol.

Q: What is a sprench?

A: A sprench is a hybrid spray drench. You mix a foliar rate like you would for spraying the canopy, then irrigate so the media is wet. You can then spray the canopy and the tops of containers, allowing you to address both canopy pests and root zone pests in one application. By acclimating to the environment, efficacy goes up.

Q: How often should we sprench?

A: Start with AzaGuard on Monday (or at the start of the rotation), and give a day in between sprenches. On Wednesday, use BioCeres, and on Friday, use Venerate or Grandevo, PFR 97, or mycoinsecticides. Keep your finger on the button and put pressure on insects while rotating different microbial actions so they don't become resistant to any one application. There has never been any documented mutation resistance to AzaGuard, which is why I recommend starting with that. It messes with their ability to feed, grow, and lay eggs.

Q: Does chitin elicit ISR?

A: Some studies suggest that it does, and products like Oxiphos or Regalia can be great tools. This is why lush agricultural areas are often near coastal spots and why compost can be a good source of chitin.

Q: What is the recommended rate for media cleanse?

A: For a preemptive media cleanse, use a 1:500-1:256 dilution rate, which is 7-15ml per gallon. For peat, coco, or soil that are susceptible to pythium and root rot, you can use a 1:100 (37ml) dilution rate, but only do it once to achieve the control you are looking for. Then, back down to a maintenance rate and keep the media clean.

Q: What are the sprench rates for large outdoor farms?

A: The sprench application volume for large outdoor farms should be 150-250 gallons per acre. When looking at the label, note that pints per acre always refer to 100 gallons, which helps you do the math. For example, if the label recommends 4 pints per acre, that would be equivalent to a 4/100 dilution rate, or 2/5, 1/25, etc. For smaller environments, you can adjust the dilution accordingly.

Q: How can I control springtails in my growing media?

A: While springtails are not harmful to plants and can indicate a healthy soil environment, if you wish to control them, you can use products like AzaGuard, BioCeres, and diatomaceous earth (DE) which are effective against soft-bodied insects. However, keep in mind that springtails are part of a healthy rhizosphere, and if you see them in your growing media, it means that you have a thriving biosphere. So, it is recommended to monitor them instead of being concerned about them.

Q: Can you tell me more about Lost Coast Plant Therapy?

A: Lost Coast Plant Therapy is a soybean-based 25B insecticide that contains citric acid and some ISO. It is recommended to be used in rotation with other products, as it only has one mode of action, which is suffocation of insects. By using a rotation like AzaGuard on Monday, a biological insecticide that is rated for spider mites on Wednesday, and Lost Coast Plant Therapy on Friday, you would be able to effectively target the population of pests while not relying solely on Plant Therapy. If the insect does not come in contact with the product, it will not be effective.

Q: Can Nuke 'Em be used as a citric base?

A: Nuke 'Em is a good product, similar to Dr. Zymes, and both contain 0.03 citric acid. Depending on your local grow store, I would recommend going with the cheaper price tag between the two.

Q: What to use to treat PM?

A: OxiPhos, ZeroTol, or citric acid (during late flower) are effective treatments for powdery mildew. Using anything else could be detrimental to the final product. Additionally, increasing airflow and eliminating temperature and humidity swings can help prevent powdery mildew.

Q: How does BioSafe compare to ProKure?

A: ProKure is a chlorine dioxide product that's very effective, especially for the cure stage. However, instead of ProKure, I recommend checking out Garden Clean, which is also a chlorine dioxide product but is more reliable for thoroughly disinfesting an environment. It's run by Javal Vias, an industry veteran, who has a lot of love for the industry.

While chlorine dioxide is effective, it's a short-lived chemistry and may not be enough to thoroughly disinfest an environment. To get the best results, I recommend using Sanidate 5 or ZeroTol to disinfest the environment and then following up with a CLO2 packet to keep any pathogens, bacteria, or spores from reemerging.

Both BioSafe and ProKure are complementary and have different applications. I recommend using both whenever possible to get the best results possible.

Q: Can you put Sanidate in your wet wall?

A: The wet wall specifications should be checked, but some growers have had good results using Sanidate at the initial treatment phase, especially if there is bioburden or mineral scale already accumulated.

This should be run for a day or two to break everything loose, and then switch to a water treatment rate. It's important to use PAA test strips to monitor the PAA levels in the wet wall. For water treatment, Sanidate is very effective against filamentous algae, cyno bacteria, zoo spore, and other organisms. By using the appropriate treatment, there should be a significant reduction in the incidence of outbreaks in the wet wall, but it's important to ensure that it's clean first.

Q: Is ZeroTol safe and effective for PM in late flower?

A: Yes, it is definitely effective for disinfesting mildew and mycelium. We recommend using it on the day of harvest so that you harvest a disinfested crop. Use a 1% solution, which means 1:100, or 37ml per gallon.

Q: Where do I find a foamer for a smaller scale garden?

A: You can call Kip at 1.888.273.3088, extension 225. He will be able to get you hooked up with our 2.6 gallon foamer, which runs about $300. Please note that equipment availability relies on the global economy, but BioSafe chemistries are US-based.

Q: What is the benefit of a foamer vs. a fogger for home grower?

A: The best part of a foamer is the adhesion that you are going to be able to achieve with it. A fogger is a very small particle and while it will disperse through an environment very fluently, the foam is going to allow you to visually confirm that you've cleaned everything and get you the contact time that you need with disinfest products. Contact is key, so if we think about a very small droplet adhering to a wall, how long does that take to evaporate? If it's only a minute or two, you probably aren't disinfesting the grow room to the fullest extent that you could be, and so it's almost like a waste of product at that point. Whereas when you can apply something as a foam and it is going to hold that chemistry there for an extended period of time, you're going to make sure that you have made the adhesion that you need, you've got the contact time that is required to disinfest your grow properly. A fogger is okay, but a foamer, talking sanitary purposes alone, the foamer is much better for you and can also double as a pesticide applicator for things like AzaGuard, Oxiphos, Zerotol, Pyrethrin, Sulfur, Insecticidal soap, the list goes on. I wouldn't really use any microbials with it, but the foamer is tech that if you are not on it yet, you should be.

Q: What would you do for alternating SOP for Root aphids?

A: I would start out with azadirachtin because of the fact it will take away the food source, take away the ability to grow, and weaken them. Make sure that when you are going after root aphids, you are doing an application method called a sprench because there's going to be some that are in your root zone, and chances are that if there are any in the canopy in that second n-star stage, they are moving around in the plants. And so what we are trying to do is basically take away their ability to molt, take away their food source, take away their ability to lay eggs, and by weakening them with that Monday approach, then on Wednesdays you'd apply something like an Evergreen Specialty which is a pyrethrin that has a chemigation rate so that you can legally put it in your root zone, then follow up with the BioCeres WP, then something like the Venerate or Grandevo. There are a ton of products out there that are very effective against them; it's just making sure that Mondays you weaken, Wednesdays you use a different heavy hitter so basically you need four of them (so every Wednesday you can rotate), and then Fridays rotating between like an SOS209 and a Nuke 'Em (25B just to keep the pressure on) so that those root aphids aren't able to have unchecked growth and get out of control.

Q: What is the best way to water indoor plants?

A: The best way to water indoor plants really depends on the type of plant and its specific watering needs. In general, it is important to water the plant thoroughly, making sure that the water penetrates deep into the soil. You can do this by watering until water starts to drain out of the bottom of the pot, indicating that the soil is fully saturated. It is also important to allow the soil to dry out slightly between waterings to prevent over-watering, which can lead to root rot and other issues.

Some plants prefer to be watered from the bottom, by placing the pot in a tray of water and allowing the water to be absorbed from the drainage holes. This is especially helpful for plants that are prone to root rot or that prefer consistently moist soil.

Another important factor to consider when watering indoor plants is the type of water you use. Tap water can contain chlorine and other chemicals that can harm plants over time, so it may be beneficial to use filtered or distilled water instead.

Overall, the key to watering indoor plants is to pay attention to the individual needs of each plant and adjust your watering schedule accordingly.

Q: Has there been any study on the effectiveness of OxiPhos to treat Hop Latent Viroid?

A: Unfortunately, we don't have any studies as of yet. However, I do have anecdotal evidence from growers who have seen much less instance of dudding when Oxiphos has been brought into the rotation. Having that plant defense system activated and ready to go, I think really does, I don't want to say eliminate, but it suppresses some of the symptoms that growers are seeing in terms of no potency, no growth, very tight, smaller structure, smaller leaves. So, again, I can't claim it is effective against HLV other than the anecdotal evidence from growers who have told me they've seen much less instance of the virus pressure when it's employed.

CLEAN GROWING: INTEGRATED PEST MANAGEMENT FOR CANNABIS GROWERS

Q: Is it worth running mykos when running tap and beneficials?

A: Yes, you will see a benefit of those because of the amount of chlorine in municipal tap water, but it's not enough to completely sterilize your water column. The best way to describe it is: would you feel safe putting a scoop of mykos in a cup and drinking it? Probably not. So, I mean, use that mentality. If you wouldn't drink it, it's probably going to be sufficient for the plant.

Q: What's the difference between BioCeres and Botaniguard?

A: The main difference is the subspecies. Botaniguard 22 WP is GHA subspecies, whereas BioCeres is an ANTO3 subspecies. The ANTO3 subspecies has larger sporangia, which means larger spores and more instances of an insect coming in contact with it, making it a better product. Another main difference is that BioCeres is OMRI listed, whereas Mycotrol is not, but the soy carrier in Mycotrol can be gunky and clogs sprayers. BioCeres also has a UV inhibitor, which means that the bacillus degrade much more slowly when exposed to light. This results in closer to 12 hours of activity for a spore, making it a great product for anyone battling aphids, whiteflies, thrips, and soft-bodied insects.

Q: Can you tank mix ZeroTol with AzaGuard and OxiPhos?

A: It's recommended to tank mix AzaGuard but not Azamax since it uses ethanol-based ingredients. AzaGuard is a good option for tank mix compatibility and cost-effectiveness.

Q: What is the right ratio per gallon for foliar application of ZeroTol?

A: For pre-harvest, use a firehose rate of 37 ml per gallon. For maintenance, use 15 ml per gallon. Make sure to mix with a buffer and RO water to reach a 0.3 EC solution. Add pH Up to neutralize the chemistry. It's recommended to spike RO water with a tenth of NPK.

Q: What rate do we apply BioCeres and how often?

A: Depending on the number of products you have in rotation, it's recommended to apply BioCeres at least twice a month on Wednesdays at a rate of 9-12 grams per gallon. This has proven to be effective for cannabis-related pests.

Q: What are some tips for using BioCeres WP?

A: When dealing with root aphids, it's recommended to do an irrigation ahead of time to get the media wet and gaslamp the bugs so that they don't run away. Root aphids are fast and can easily outrun any moisture or treatment. Once they are acclimated to a moist environment, follow up with a sprayer and hit the canopy, then do a 1-4 1000 count depending on the size of your media to get the chemistry into the root ball. Use 9-12 grams per gallon of BioCeres WP and apply in the morning with the lights turned off above the row being sprayed. This will help to hit the root aphids where they live and provide the efficacy you're looking for.

Q: Are BioSafe products a must for a coco home grower?

A: For Home and Hobby growers, we would recommend looking into:

1. TerraGrow - This will do very well in coco-based media. It has 5 bacillus strains, trichoderma, kelp and humic acid, so it will save you money on other supplements. Plus, you're not going to need to buy enzymes because it has enzymatic qualities that it produces, so you're not going to need to supplement with something that's got competitive microbes in it like endo mycorrhizae and trichoderma. They will eat each other if there is no pathogen present, which is why they tell you to use such high rates. and charge you such a high amount. TerraGrow in Denver for a 4lb container retails for about $80, and you use it at a half gram to a gram per gallon. We are here for the grower. We are not trying to get you guys to buy a bunch of filler. We just want to make sure that what you are using is efficient.
2. ZeroTol HC - We recommend looking into this as well. That's the ZeroTol size for the home grower. Basically it's a gallon size but once you get the HC you will probably upgrade to the 2.0 because you can use it to clean your trays, your tables,

your pots, your plants, your root zone, your irrigation. ZeroTol is a very versatile product so that's definitely a must.

3. OxiPhos - Lastly, I would recommend integrating OP as well because if you can boost the immunity of your plants and not have a weak one in your herd, you are basically setting yourself up for less problems down the road.

Q: How often should I apply TerraGrow to coco?

A: For transplant, use a slurry of 3oz per 10 gallons, dunking the whole root ball to establish a good initial colony. After that, depending on your media, use half a gram to one gram per gallon bi-weekly. For high CEC media with a lot of humus, use one gram per gallon, and for inert media like Grodan, use half a gram per gallon. Coco falls somewhere in the middle, so both rates can work, and you'll have to figure out which is most economical for you as a grower.

Q: What's the difference between TerraGrow and TerraClean?

A: TerraGrow is a microbial inoculant containing 5 strains of bacillus, as well as licheniformis and magitariam, kelp, humic, and biostimulant. TerraClean, on the other hand, is a peroxide and PAA product used to deal with soil-borne root diseases such as fusarium, pythium, phytophthora, and saccharomyces. The best way to use both products is to start with TerraClean to clean the soil, then use TerraGrow to reintroduce beneficial microbes, and then plant and grow.

Q: Do you need PPE when doing IPM?

A: Yes, it is recommended to wear proper personal protective equipment (PPE) when handling professional-grade chemicals like ZeroTol, Sanidate, and OxiPhos. Eye protection is especially important as getting these chemicals in your eyes can cause blindness. Always read labels for dedicated PPE.

Q: Any issues with breathing in BioCeres WP?

A: Yeah, don't do it. On the label, it clearly states that adequate respirator requirements are necessary. BioCeres WP is a fungus that grows in damp dark soil and an ounce of prevention is worth a pound of cure. Please don't breathe in BioCeres WP, as it kills stuff, mainly insects, but let's not test it on humans. Using an N95 respirator is a good idea.

Q: Will BioCeres kill nematodes?

A: AzaGuard would be better. If you are utilizing nematodes, do a ZeroTol+AG application on monday, BioCeres on Wednesday, and then add your nematodes on Friday.

Q: How do you get the foamer to suds up like in a car wash? Having trouble dialing in.

A: Make sure you are mixing a biofoaming agent at 120ml per gallon to ensure there's enough foaming agent in there. If your mixing ratios are correct, then your compressor is too small.

If you are using one of those hand pump compressors, I really recommend investing in one of those little pancake ones—a little Senco works great and saves you from looking like 1-arm popeye.

Two most common issues that can cause it to not foam up:

1. Not enough foaming agent.
2. Compressor isn't sufficient - shooting for 40psi or 1.5bar.

Q: What pests can you use AzaGuard for?

A: AzaGuard is good for pretty much any pests, with 300 species of insects listed. AzaGuard regulates growth, takes away food and eggs, but it needs a knockdown.

Q: How about BTnow for outdoor?

A: Regarding BTnow for outdoor use, it is BTK (bacillus thuringiensis kurstaki) which is an antifeedant that can be applied to plants.

Caterpillars ingest the BTK crystals, and it creates a protein A enzyme that's a stop feeding action, and it shuts down the caterpillar's digestive system. Even though you might not see dead caterpillars on day 1, you're going to see damage to your canopy go from maximum to minimal.

Within 3-5 days, you will see dead caterpillar bodies. It's a very good tool for later on once your plants start to set, because if you see corn earworm, chances are you're going to see botrytis as well. Therefore, because it is a later flower application, it is

216

recommended to do a pre-harvest spray with ZeroTol to mitigate any residual active spore that could be present and address any botrytis that could be there. For best results, mix it with a nonionic surfactant like coco wet or natural wet.

Q: Can you Use BTNow for larvae like mosquitos and root aphids?

A: BTK subspecies is for caterpillars and is not labeled for mosquitos or root aphids.

Acknowledgements

Zac:

I'd like to thank my parents and my beautiful wife Ali for encouraging me to follow my dreams. The gardening unlimited crew for helping me learn. Bio Safe for allowing me to become the "Grow Guy." ACW for allowing me to compile tons of knowledge. ALL MY GROWMIES, without you this wouldn't be possible. Ben for writing my thoughts down on paper. And thank you, the reader, who cares about their crops.

Ben:

I'd like to thank my family for their incredible support throughout my journey in this space—as both a writer and cannabis professional. Thank you to my parents, Mike & Susan, my sister, Emily, and my wife, Jordan for encouraging my passions and celebrating the results. Thank you to Cole Mather for always pushing me to achieve and create more as a writer. Thank you to Colin Gordon for introducing me to Zac and his vast amount of knowledge. Thank you to Zac for trusting me to curate and present your knowledge to the world. And thank you, the reader of this book, for wanting to grow cleaner cannabis, for investing in your craft, and for buying this book.

219

IPM Index

A

B

C

D

Q

227

R

S

T

U

V

W

Y

Z

Made in the USA
Coppell, TX
06 January 2024

27351412R00128